THE KILLING GAMES

THE KILLING GAMES

By Angie Riedel

THE DOT CONNECTOR LIBRARY, BOOK 4

Published by Paul Bondarovski

Selected, edited and published by Paul Bondarovski © 2016.
Publisher's website: www.wariscrime.com.

Text and cover design by Paul Bondarovski.

ISBN 978-1-53684-102-2

Contents

From the publisher

This is the second collection of Angie Redel's incredible essays and the book 4 of the *Dot Connector Library* series. Some of the articles that you will find here had been written and/or edited by the author for the *Dot Connector Magazine* that I had been publishing and where I hoped to convince Angie to become the chief editor. She never said no, but she wasn't someone to irresponsibly say yes either, without being sure she would find enough forces to invest herself in the project full-time. That's the way she lived and worked. She was excited by the idea of publishing her articles in a book, but said that some of them still require editing and some 'final touch'. All taking care to leave her unique writing style intact, I did this editing and 'final touch' work. Hope Angie would have approved and be happy with the result.

Angie Riedel's essays, if not life-changing, are definitely mind-changing and are must-read for all freethinking or simply thinking readers.

Paul Bondarovski,
August 2016

Everything we know is wrong.
It's the best-kept secret out there.
The truth is that life is threatened
in a world controlled by greed and power.
It's time to wake up, rise up, and recreate
the world that deserves to exist.
A place of peace, equality, and creativity
that forever strives to become
the best of all possibilities.

Dominated to Death

A mentality of total domination has taken over the significant power points that run our world. It is taking us into total destruction, and we know it. The time has come to choose: authoritarianism to total destruction or independent minds for continued existence and peace. Pick one.

Do we really want to see the end of the world? Are we supposed to quietly sit back and let a sick authoritarian system dominate us and take us literally to the end of all life on earth? Do we really support the mindless pollution of our necessary resources? Should anyone be considered entitled to pollute our air, water and soil for profit and leave us no means to keep ourselves and our future children alive and healthy? Who has the right to decide for everyone else that they can take it all and we don't get a voice? There is no such person or country or organization.

No one owns our world or has the right to call any shots for anyone except themselves. We all own the planet, because we're a part of it. It belongs to us. Its resources belong to all of us and they are there, free for the taking.

The earth sustains us, it always has. It's our birth right. Who has the right to decide it won't support life anymore? We need clean air, pure water and unadulterated natural food to sustain our lives. These are not optional, they are required, and without them we will die.

Air is the most critical, because we will die within minutes without it. That makes it pretty darn important, even without a scientific study to back it up. It's obvious and just the kind of thing that 'experts' take forever to figure out when everyone else already knows it.

Water is the next most important concern, because we can go without food for weeks, but we cannot go without water more than a few days. Water must be pure and clean, because it cleanses our bodies. It's the rinse cycle of our amazingly complex inner workings. It washes out toxins and dead cells, it hydrates our organs, eyes and brains, it keeps our skin healthy and beautiful, our lips free of cracking and peeling. It's a very important part of staying alive and healthy, and it too is not optional. We will perish without it.

Real natural food is the only thing that can feed our living bodies. Real food is alive. We eat life to maintain life. Food has been real and natural for tens of thousands of years, it is all our bodies know, and it is all they need. From food our bodies can build themselves, they can draw whatever raw materials they need to affect healing and repairs and keep us healthy and energetic. The bulk of natural foods is used to keep our natural plumbing clean and free of clogs, and that's no small thing. Fiber is gentle enough to go through our system, but abrasive enough to scrub the colon walls, removing parasites, toxins and other kinds of build-ups that would ultimately lead to our getting sick, diseased and dying far too soon.

Air, water and food are not optional. They are the most basic three things that everyone needs in order to stay alive and to have and maintain real, vigorous health. To the extent they are poisoned, degraded, toxic and artificial is the extent we are not getting our most basic needs met. We will obviously begin to suffer ill health and a variety of diseases. We will grow weaker, dumber, less energetic, less able to navigate through life effectively. Our children will be born weaker, smaller and less able to thrive.

Earth provides all of its life forms with what they need to survive and thrive. Every creature needs clean water and air and safe natural food sources. We have always had these things, and they have sustained our species for thousands upon thousands of years.

But today there is no place on earth, no matter how remote, that doesn't have traces of man-made toxic chemicals in the lakes and rivers and streams, or in the ice in remote Antarctica, or in the air that everything must breathe.

The air and water in our cities and homes is a nightmare of crud and filth. The nuclear energy and bombs our government is so profoundly in love with have decimated our best farm lands all over the country, because the factories that make this nuclear death soup are not safe, they are not sound. They leak, and they irradiate our rivers and our soil, and the radioactive particles settle on the ground, go into our food, and we eat them. We breathe them. We are dying from them. We are all in a constant bath of toxic gases and liquids, pesticides and biochemical concoctions, and, of course, the nightmare of radioactivity, which poisons an area and cannot be cleaned up. It turns entire cities and vast acres of fertile farm land into desolate wastelands of death that will continue to kill for billions of years.

Who on earth has the right and the privilege to decide to destroy precious dwindling farm lands, poison once pristine rivers and lakes, and combine the genes of foreign species for our food without our knowledge or consent? Is there a human being in the world who has this entitlement? Is there someone walking amongst us whose rightful call it is to determine that some will die for the sake of industry, without warning them or even telling them to move, without helping them as they slowly perish in frustration, legal costs, and finally lose everything?

Who is it that calls these shots? Wouldn't we all like to have a chat with this Mr. So Important Person? What makes him so special? What entitles him to spread D.U. all around the Middle East and allow its particulates to be carried in the wind to literally every corner of the world?

Who decided that economies and corporations were the top dogs of planet Earth and that money is power and with it comes a world of special power and privilege? When some very few people with incomprehensible wealth hoard ill-gotten trillions they'll never need or use or want, how does this translate into making them the right kind of people to run the entire world? What are their qualifications? Business acumen is not a qualifier, business has nothing to do with what humanity needs or cares about. Money is not a qualifier, it's a tool. If I had a million hammers, could I run your life? I don't think so. Money is not an entitlement to more of everything than anyone else can have. It is not a blanket free ride to buy our government out from under us and subordinate us to whatever whims and goals they might possess. Money has nothing to do with the person who has it. They are not their money. Money, in fact, is one of the most irrelevant things in the world. If it all disappeared tomorrow, we would all be fine.

We would all be fine, because the vast majority of us have very little of it, and we're used to that. It would only be the greatest nightmare of all time for a couple dozen twisted old white men who have more of it than even makes sense. More than they could use in a thousand lifetimes of regal high living. Men who are so obsessed with money and wealth and getting more that they are dysfunctional human beings, disconnected from the meaning and value of life.

These men aren't the natural choice to decide the fates of billions of human beings and all of the life forms on land, in the sea, and in the air. They aren't interested in anything that doesn't bring them more wealth and power. They see the earth in terms of digging it up for its resources and leaving it broken and destroyed. They don't care about the pollution of their gigantic industrial complexes, they care only about profits and growth. They don't lose any sleep over newborn babies with over 200 industrial chemicals already present in their bodies. They don't care about the state of health dropping drastically from the poison and garbage they package as edibles and take no responsibility for. When we grow obese from their artificial fat-laden foods, our arteries clog, our bodies get sick, and their pharmaceutical plants churn out expensive drugs to help us lose weight and keep us on refills for the rest of our lives in order to keep our overburdened hearts from bursting in our chests.

They run commercials to shame us for our poor health and weight gain, and they parade out skinny models who look like they're at death's door, and they tell us, "Look, this is what you should look like. If you don't look like this, you're a fat pig and should feel great shame. It's all your fault that you're sick and tired and overwhelmed. It's all your fault that life is nothing more than getting up in the morning to the sound of an alarm and going off to work for us so we can get wealthy off your labor."

These are the men who look at war and its machines as so very profitable. They like war, it's great for business. So what if millions die, they all had to die someday. "The important thing is that we get very, very rich every time there's a clash. In fact, whenever possible we enjoy getting those clashes going. It's only business, it's nothing personal."

Excuse me, but I have to disagree. This is about as personal as it gets.

More and more we are able to clearly see that a certain mindset is invading our world, and it's changing our lives, but not for the better. Who these people are and what their game plan is, we don't know. But we do know what we can see with our own eyes, and what we are seeing is alarming. Things are past the point of critical. We are truly being threatened, our very survival is tenuous, precariously balanced on the tip of some fat cat's cigar. International unrest makes no sense, we're all people, and we all want peace. We don't want these wars, we don't want to fund all of these horrible weapons, and we don't want to live in fear. None of us chose what these players have put into motion, and nothing is standing up to stop them. They are cutting away all of the restrictions that used to bind them and keep them from doing exactly what they're doing now. Our military is weak and bankrupt, lacking the most basic things it needs to protect us. Our police force is becoming ever more militarized, and swat teams are used to deliver simple warrants, often with terrible damage being done to innocent people. We have a president who finds Geneva suddenly too "vague" to be able to pin down its intent, though no one before him has expressed any inability to grasp its purpose.

We have a country bowing down to total domination in the name of safety and protection. It is wholly unconcerned with the loss of our God-given rights, the imprisonment of citizens without a warrant, without evidence and without the legal right to a lawyer. Everything we stand for has been systematically disassembled and laid at our feet with a smirk, and no one's phone calls or emails bypass the national security mechanism. We are all a threat to the state, and today none of us are safe in our own homes anymore. The biggest threat of all is our own government's domination and the growing belief in our population that this is how it should be.

Total submission to the will of authority, unquestioning obedience and total support of the government. We worship the 'experts' they condone and we believe that doctors are infallible and only concerned with our well-being. We believe the talk show hosts and the television news, and if they say they are fair and balanced, then we know it must be true. They would never lie to us.

For those of us who are not swept up in this authoritarian takeover of America and its values what we see playing out around us is frightening. We know where this will lead. We know that, if left unchecked, it will keep getting worse until it gets so bad that everything and everyone is threatened.

Those who are caught up in it are vocal supporters filled with hate and recriminations, they dismiss facts and ignore reason. For them obedience is the mark of a true American, and no wrong can be done when we obey our Commander In Chief. No matter how it looks, no matter how hopeless it seems, no matter how many people have died, if he says stay the course and do the surge, they are there. All that's missing is a rousing cry of 'Heil Hitler'.

We have to face the scariest truth of all time. These people are in control and they now have the technology to wipe every living thing off the face of the earth. And the thought of total annihilation doesn't seem to bother them. Their total disconnect from reality may scare the pants off us, but to them it feels like perfection. It is God's will. The end justifies the means, we can do no wrong, and we must win at all costs.

They are insane. We are in danger. And we know they must be stopped. We have to face that, and we have to decide which way it's going to go. Who is going to steer this ship, them or us? We either have to choose to fall in with their lockstep and become one of the hive-minded true believers who are willing to blow the planet to smithereens and wait for Jesus; or we have to realize that these people don't have the right to destroy this perfect, beautiful, irreplaceable world, or to determine our future, or to deny our right to live in peaceful prosperity without war and violence and profiting off the deaths of innocents. It doesn't have to be this way. It's not up to them. But if we want it stopped, it's up to us to stop them.

If we don't speak up, it's the same as saying, "Help yourselves." It's permission.

The time has come to choose. There is a moment ahead where the choice will no longer exist. It will pass, and it will be gone forever. Untold horror is guaranteed to follow, and we know this. We have to choose and we have to do whatever it takes to get these crazies back into their cages where they can be true believers all they like without hurting anyone else. Tell your family, tell your friends, and spread the reality around where everyone can see it. This is it. Choose. What's it gonna be? War or peace? Domination or freedom? Mind control or free thought? Cooperation or force? Money for weapons or money for helping humans?

Print up flyers. Talk about it at the bar. Let's get it into public discourse, and we better make the most of the time. We can do this. All that needs to happen is that people realize that we're on the brink. And don't ever buy into the idea that we're powerless, that's a total lie. We outnumber them by hundreds of millions, and our power lies in working like termites to undermine their power and take out the floor from underneath them. Talk about it. Everything that ever happened started by talking about it. We can all do that.

Tuesday, February 20, 2007.

One and One is One

I'm not impressed with george w. bush or his supposed deep connection to Christianity. Either the man is an all-out liar and fraud, or he's absolutely the stupidest 'leader' of the century. I'm going with fraud. He's no rocket scientist, but the amount of damage he's done has far exceeded any possible accident, ineptitude, or stupidity. He knows exactly what he's doing. And to get it done, he lies. Fraud is the man's M.O.

He uses religion as a costume and mask to hide behind, believing that if he keeps asserting his heartfelt belief in God that people will see that to the exclusion of all else and that they will believe everything he's doing is sanctified. They will see his religiosity and say, "There goes a Godly man." They will excuse his every flaw, even the worst ones, believing that because he professes his love of Christ that he must be honest and he must be trustworthy. They will not ask themselves how it can be that everything the man does is in direct conflict to his supposed religious beliefs, they will excuse his errant behavior. Somehow in their minds, if people see bush as a strong Christian, it will mean he can do no wrong.

Why do people believe that Christians can do no wrong? Who do they suppose our prisons are filled with? They are filled with Christians. Christians who lie, cheat and steal. Christians who murder.

Come on, people, get over yourselves. Just because someone says he's a Christian doesn't mean he can't be a lying, cheating criminal. This knee-jerk belief that a Christian leader can do no wrong is both naive and supremely arrogant, and it's not just hurting the credibility of the Christians, it's doing irreversible damage to our country and countless

people in other countries. Particularly the countries gw bush has decided to invade and crush to death to keep us 'safe'.

I'm not a Christian, but I'm also not a stranger to the Bible. I've studied it, I've actually read it, and I'm with Gandhi when he expressed this opinion: "I like your Christ, I do not like your Christians. Your Christians are so unlike your Christ." There is more truth to this than a lot of Christians want to face.

How can I say that? Well, let's turn it around, and why don't you tell me how Christian it is for a leader to do any of the following:

- torture people;
- break treaties that are in place to protect human rights;
- turn his back on the people to serve the sole interests of corporations at our expense;
- allow tens of millions to go without access to medical and dental care;
- betray us with lies about a growing economy that is actually teetering on the brink of total collapse;
- call for wars on false grounds and kill over a million innocent people;
- swear to uphold the law and then circumvent it at every opportunity.

I can read as well as anyone, and what I can tell you without doubt is this: If Christ were president, none of the above would ever have happened. But it's safe to say that we will never have Christ in the oval office, and frankly, I think it's obvious it's the last place he would have any interest in being. Jesus Christ had no time for the trappings of the glitterati of power, wealth and government. He spent all of his time with regular people and he worked to feed the hungry, heal the sick, get rid of demons and overthrow the cheating, thieving money changers. He forgave Judas for betraying him to the government. He did not take up arms. Ever. He was a teacher and a peace maker, standing up for what is right in the face of a mob mentality that supported the state in all of its iniquity.

Jesus made it perfectly clear what he thought of government power. When people came to him and asked him about whether or not to pay taxes to Caesar, Jesus said a whole lot in one sentence: "Render unto Caesar that which is Caesar's, and render unto God that which is God's." He wasn't just talking about paying taxes. He was talking about the whole government and power thing. How much are we supposed to give the government? According to Christ's own words, the government and God are not connected, they are not the same. He makes the distinction plainly in that one sentence. God and government are two completely different things, and Jesus never even suggested that there was any such thing as a middle ground where they connected, he knew better than that. Christ wasn't telling the public to obey the government and pay taxes. What he was saying was that the government is a powerful force that can and definitely will mess you up if you don't do what it demands. That's just reality. The government killed Christ, in case anyone missed that part. No single person can stand up to government power, take it on, and expect to come out in one piece. Not even Jesus Christ could make them be decent people who respected God.

I always read Christ's response to mean, "Do what you have to do to keep the state satisfied, but then get back to doing what really matters: God's work." He did specify to also render unto God that which is God's, and then he lived the example of how that's done. He blew off the government otherwise, but knew full well it was there. He didn't waste his time dinking with it, because it didn't matter to him. He knew they were power-hungry thugs who loved money, and he meant to keep his focus on what mattered to him. The example he made was in the hopes of teaching others the same. Do what you have to do, but keep doing God's work.

Did I get any of that wrong? I don't think so. I'll ask again then, what is so Godly about gw bush? Since he came into power, illegally, due to subverting the vote, he has changed the fabric of America into dirty laundry. He has used illegal, heavy-handed tactics to force his will on this country every bit as much as he's done abroad. This man has no respect for human life, for our lives, for anyone's life in the Middle East. How can anyone be responsible for the deaths of over a million people and not feel sick to their soul? What on earth is worth that price? I really want to know. You tell me.

There's nothing worth having that comes at the cost of genocide and destruction of countries. What on earth do we believe he's doing over there? If we are too arrogant to ever step outside ourselves and see ourselves as others see us, then we will continue this deadly charade of hypocrisy. We are perfectly capable of engaging in every kind of wrongdoing that humanity is capable of, and it's high time we got that through our heads. I don't care how Christian anyone claims to be; if their actions are the opposite of how Christ would act, then they're frauds.

If they hate people just because they look or speak different, wear different clothes or have different cultures, then they are bigots. They are not like Christ at all. If they want war and more war, they are war mongers and nothing like the Christ they claim to love. If they support torture, rape and pillage and ignore their leader's obvious attempts to defraud the people, then they are hypocrites. They are not patriots, they are not Christians, they are fooling themselves, anxious to serve a crooked human master. They want to worship a man, not God.

God gave them eyes to see with and minds of their own and expects them to use those things wisely. To not be blind followers of such obviously corrupt loathsome leadership. To not ignore the suffering this leader's policies are causing both at home and abroad.

I expect Christians to be amongst the most tolerant, kind, forgiving people on this earth, but are they? Are they supporting bush's torture tactics? Are they happily laying down to allow an abusive government to destroy every freedom we once had?

As I said, I'm not a Christian, but I have every right to be here and live my life, every bit as much as Christians do. Certain Christians, like bush, believe that living on this earth is their right alone, and they're wrong about that. This is not their private world, it is filled with billions of others, and they have to share it. They must also strive to get along with those others and to not accept policies of a government that insists that the only way to keep us safe is to aggressively attack other countries and wage wars without cause or provocation of any kind. That's not even sane, much less Christian.

I've had to learn tolerance for all of the religiosity around me, and I have. It wasn't hard. But when exactly will it be a two-way street? When will Christians begin to show acceptance of those who are not in their private club? When will the Christians begin to share the planet and show some of Christ's love for the other peoples of the world and for their own countrymen?

We all have the right to our own beliefs and values, it's not up to the Christians or any other group. It's not up to the government, or the Zionists, or the corporations, or the neocons, or the right, or the left, or the political bullies on the airwaves and in Congress, or the other bullies behind the scenes guiding the mentality of total control by force into the public mind. Freedom means the individual right to have one's own beliefs and to live them without being relentlessly attacked, attacked to death. Nobody's gang is right to abuse anyone else. There's a very old saying, "Live and let live." What else is there?

For Christians who are also Americans, you'd think they above all others would understand that and sincerely support it. Not just for themselves, but for everyone. Bush doesn't do that. Freedom is not in contradiction with Christianity, but bigotry, intolerance and hate are. So is war. So is attacking people for having different points of view in politics or religious beliefs. So are small-minded petty assertions that somehow you're special and no one else is. We're all in this together, no matter what any group may believe.

Some beliefs are just wrong. They're wrong even though they're widely accepted and familiar to everyone. Just because something is widely accepted doesn't make it true. It just makes it widely accepted. It used to be widely accepted that the world was flat. If you were alive back then and said otherwise, you'd have run into some serious trouble. Another belief that's long overdue some correction is almost as old as the flat earth belief, but it's still in full swing. It's the notion of 'God and country'.

Somehow these two totally unrelated opposite things have been laid side by side so closely they became one thing. But there is no such thing. The phrase evokes immediate images of a waving flag and parades and patriotism, and it brings up strong feelings of righteousness and honor. All of the things it evokes are about war. The phrase is used specifically to get people to support wars they would not otherwise support. Who needs slogans when your home is under attack? If we were being attacked or invaded, we wouldn't hesitate to pick up arms and defend ourselves. It's not about apple pie and glory then, it's a reality that you either fight to defend your own life and property or you die and lose it all.

'God and country' means supporting wars of aggression, and it's used time and again with other mind games like 'support the troops'. That one means 'support the war of aggression or you won't be supporting your own families abroad killing strangers and being killed by strangers'. It seeks to make you look and feel like you're unpatriotic, when the fact is you just don't support bogus wars of aggression. How about supporting the truth for a change?

There is nothing in either of those phrases that have one single thing to do with God. What's the God part of 'God and country'? There is no God part. What a deceitful phrase it is. Think about it. God has nothing to do with country.

This phrase was constructed by skilled practitioners of social engineering, devised for a very specific purpose. The same purpose that gw bush constantly asserts his religiosity for. By linking God to country, or to anything else for that matter, the lines between them become blurred. Blurred to the point that there's no separation between them in the eyes of the public, and the two separate things meld into one. The public simply hears the God part and the link is automatically established. God and country become inseparable as though they're the same thing, and the people are then compelled to act as if they are the same thing. They treat the government with all of the respect, reverence, trust and obedience they'd show to God. But they aren't the same. They have nothing in common.

Just as gw bush's actions have nothing in common with Christian doctrine, God and country are not only opposites, they are in a state of perpetual conflict and competition. They're both competing for people's minds and hearts and lives.

People like to believe that their government is really truly linked to their own religious beliefs and values, and it's strongly encouraged for them to believe that. But why? Because a great deal of what government does cannot be justified. It can't stand on its own merits and be accepted by the public, because it's completely unacceptable. A lot of what government does is actually harmful to the people, face it. They take your money at gunpoint and send you off to die in wars they contrive for reasons of their own. They throw people in prison whether they're guilty or not and deprive them of their freedom, property and rights at will. They kill people. They use us for their own purposes and for personal profit long after they leave office.

In order for the government to achieve its goals they need to get the population on board. But why would anyone in their right mind accept being taxed into poverty or being shipped off to kill strangers when it's obviously not in their own best interests to agree to or go along with? They wouldn't. The government knows that and that's why it is always desperate for credibility, and this handy trick is the primo shortcut to getting that credibility.

They know very well that if they can successfully blur the lines between church and state that in very short order anything the state gets up to will be supported by the people who will have forgotten that the government is not Godlike. That distinction will be completely lost on the vast majority of the people who will then feel that it is right and noble and valid to do whatever the state demands of them. They will also feel very strongly that those who disagree with the government are disagreeing with their deeply held religious beliefs. Attacking the government becomes the same as attacking God. Disagreeing with the government makes you a traitor.

This false connection leads to a breakdown of the people's ability to think for themselves and to keep the government under control, instead allowing the government to control them. This is the goal of all government. That's just a fact.

And that is precisely why the myth of 'God and country' is the number one tactic used to get the people of any country to look to their leaders and see them as credible. Hitler did his thing after getting the people on board with the 'God and country' trick. Look at England, their royal heads of state are the 'defenders of the faith'. They aren't leaving the connections up to the imagination, they're casting them in stone in the people's minds. This is the only bastion of indelible credibility that governments have, and they are not ashamed to use it. Even our own government uses it in spite of the fact it's against our Constitution for exactly this reason.

It works exactly the same in advertising. That's why sex can sell beer. Sex can sell about anything. They just show you a scantily clad buxom babe next to any product, and boom, instant sales. And the funny thing is that the guys who rush out and buy those beers or motorcycles or whatever it is actually feel they are sexier and that scantily clad buxom babes are just around the corner for them now that they've got the product in hand. Obviously, a well-paid model in a swim suit posing next to a carburetor has nothing to do with auto parts. She will not be in the box, nor will some other pretty woman on the street feel any compulsion to date a guy with a certain brand of beer or carburetor.

We humans are strongly inclined to blur the lines between totally unrelated things simply because they are asserted to us together and then are repeated; soon we come to believe a great many falsehoods because of this, and we act on them. Such things form the core of some of our most strongly held beliefs, and the sad thing is that all the while it was contrived. It was the goal. To get you to connect one thing with another until you couldn't see them as separate anymore. Until you believe that one plus one is one.

It's not like you can accuse the advertising industry of lying. They'll never directly say, "Buy our brand of beer and get chicks." They'll show you ridiculous scenarios on the TV where beautiful girls are interacting with men who have their beer brand in hand. The suggestion is powerful, and what cements it is the emotional response the viewer has when he sees the silly ad. Consciously, he knows it's a gimmick, but those emotions inside him don't get that. They think it's real, because emotions are always real. And every time they see that brand of beer on the store shelves they'll remind the guys they want that beer because of the chicks on the TV commercials.

It's all very subtle and automatic, and in case it needs to be said, it works like crazy. But are the ads lying? Nope. You couldn't take them to court and say it's false advertising, they'd just turn it all around on you as if you're crazy for not being able to tell the difference between a six pack and a chick in a bikini. *You* would be the one being laughed out of court.

Of course, they'd know all along they got you. Yes, they entrapped you. Yes, they strongly asserted the connection. They spent hundreds of millions of dollars figuring out exactly how to hit you so hard with an emotional connection to beer and sex that you'd almost have to be abnormal to not get sucked in to some extent. It is all subconscious and nearly impossible to deflect. You can't make yourself immune from this kind of emotion-based mind control, and that's exactly what it is. It's quite insidious.

Advertisers do this for one reason and one reason only: they want your money. They are going to compel you in any way they can to get you to want to open your wallet for their products and give them your money. Not just once, but again and again and again, that's where branding comes in. They want you hooked for life, opening your wallet for them and only them every single day. They want you to be completely sucked in by their subconscious emotional hooks, because they work so well, and corporations have gotten richer than God because of it. They've achieved astounding success and they've perfected the techniques of manipulating masses of people with these emotional hooks, and all the time people don't even notice it happening.

We tend to believe that because we can consciously reject an obviously stupid message that we will not be sucked in, but that's clearly not true. The messages aren't directed at your brain, they are directed at your inner emotions, the ones you don't talk about, the ones that drive you, that you obsess about, are embarrassed about or dream about. We are totally conditioned to receive these hooks deeply into our subconscious minds and we don't even notice the hundreds of companies living inside our heads, compelling us to buy this and that, and only brand X of some make of car or another, or some brand of soda, when the fact is it just doesn't matter at all. And the rest of the fact is you don't even need or want the junk they have gotten you hooked into thinking you have to have or you just won't be okay. We buy things for reasons we don't even understand and feel like when we do, we are going to be rewarded in some way.

Look at McDonald's connecting itself to children having fun. There's nothing fun about a crappy mass-produced synthetic meat burger pumped full of chemicals. These things are not in any way related, they have nothing in common. But if you believe they are one and the same, or, more importantly, if your children believe it, then McDonald's knows you'll drag your kids out to their greasy processed junk food restaurants and fill their bodies with what amounts to cheap toxic waste. They would never dare claim their food is good for your kids. They don't care if your kids get sick, they want your money. They've found the exact formula to get it too.

The examples are endless, you can find them during every commercial. Try some of those pharmaceutical ads. Erectile dysfunction ads showing a man and a woman with the raging hots. Hmmm, somehow that pill is going to affect her too? How is that possible? Or is it? Of course not, the pill won't affect anyone but the poor schmuck who swallows it. But if he swallows it with the belief that it will make him feel sexy and desirable and that he'll be having mad passionate intercourse if he runs out and gets that prescription from his doctor, then he'll have done exactly what the ad was designed to make him do – buy a bottle of pills, because he connects them to sexual intercourse. It works every time. No questions asked, no facts necessary. Just assert that sex is yours with a bottle of this prescription and you go off asking your doctor to write you a prescription.

The government, desperate for credibility, did not miss out on this phenomenon. In fact, I suspect they probably invented it. They do it, because they want your money too, but they want a whole lot more than your money. They want everything you have, and they want you to believe that's a good thing, and even to support their agenda even though it's bad for you. They've done it.

They really know how to pull this off. They know exactly how to address the public and mix ideas like security with killing a million innocent people overseas to make the public think that the one will assure the other. But it's completely untrue. They have nothing to do with each other.

The so-called 'war on terror' is the mother of all head games. There is nothing credible or possible in the statement 'war on terror'. It's a non-thing. And that means they've lied us into paying for and engaging in unnecessary wars for reasons that only they know. It's about money and power, but it's not about ridding the world of terror and it's not about keeping anyone in this country safe. A million plus people are dead now. Are you safe yet?

In the first place, acts of terror are civilian crimes, not military attacks. They are carried out by individuals who are not connected in any formal way. They should be treated as crimes and prosecuted as crimes. What killers in our own country are tracked down by invading military forces that shoot everyone in the city in the attempt to locate and arrest a murderer? That would go against common sense, wouldn't it? If someone is in trouble for killing innocent people, then how can we go around killing innocent people ourselves in the name of arresting a killer who kills innocent people? You see, it doesn't make sense. It doesn't hold up to the slightest scrutiny. It's bull. If we're trying to save lives, we probably wouldn't be taking so many of them in the process and be suggesting it makes perfect sense to kill people in order to save them from bad guys. Good grief.

Secondly, there are specific reasons that acts of terror happen. They happen when life becomes so unbearable due to the injustice and oppression of some stronger group that they cannot take it anymore. It means there are no legal means to approach oppressors and work out equitable solutions. The oppressors aren't the least bit interested in working anything out, or any equitable anything. They want this other group gone. It means that people are being treated with such disrespect and cruelty that it literally gets to the point where they would rather die trying to fight back than to go on living on their knees. That's what it means.

If we truly want to end terrorism, then we're going about it in the worst possible way. We're adding fuel to the fire. We cannot end violence with more violence. We can only end it by addressing the problems and solving them once and for all.

The problems are easy to pinpoint. They're the same problems every-where you go and find unrest. What's missing is justice and autonomy, the right to decide your own fate and to live free from control and violence from those who don't want you to have those things. Along with that always comes the widespread lack of the most basic levels of prosperity for everyone.

These things are easy to understand. They're perfectly reasonable things to want. Everyone needs these things, or life is a very hellish experience. And all of these things are more than obtainable, but the reality is that there are those who have far more than enough, more than we can comprehend, and they don't want everyone to have what they need to survive. They'd rather let millions die so that they can have it all for themselves. So millions of people have nothing and are excluded as if they don't matter, but they do matter. This is what we need to be addressing. This is what we should be fighting for, to bring legal and economic justice to all of the areas of the world where people are being prevented from having what they need to survive and are not able to do anything about it.

When the only thing left is an act of terror, that should be something we can understand. We should be able to see it for what it is and choose to investigate all sides of any story, not just take official stories at face value. Let the other sides speak too. Let them speak for themselves and tell it as they see it, because they will see it very differently. Then we can say we have an idea of the truth, but in lieu of that, we have no truth. We're being manipulated into fighting, when that's already what the problem is. In effect, we're punishing the victims instead of helping them. We've been sold this gigantic mountain of bull puckie with the same lies that equate acts of terror with insane people who don't even deserve to be heard out, and so off we go killing people by the thousands.

Our current situation is a spectacular example of officials using mind-warping 'one and one is one' tactics to get the public on board with a private agenda of greed and power. Connecting the events of 9/11 to an aggressive military attack and invasion of two other countries really shows how good they are at this stuff. They discouraged our critical thinking immediately after 9/11. While everyone was still in shock and reeling from the blow, they stepped in and said, "Look to us now, you're in terrible danger and you need us to save you. You must trust us and do whatever we say. If you do, then we can protect you from the evil people. Stay terrified, but go shopping and just do whatever we say, or you will all die horrible deaths." And the traumatized public said, "Okay."

The government then immediately launched into its own ready-made game plan, safe in the knowledge that it was now a belief amongst the public that everything they were doing would be for our own safety and security, and they've played this as far as it can go. If anyone criticizes their obvious illegal acts or points out their nonsensical logic, those persons are simply attacked and accused of wanting another terror attack to happen.

It's easy to whip up a whole lot of hysteria with this game, and a whole lot of other stuff too. In reality, this country is being used as a big dumb obedient thug with a giant club to pound helpless people into submission or just to death in order to allow a small group of corporate greed mongers to get us off to a hundred year war to make weapons sellers futures bright for a long time to come. Just look at who's been raking in the hundreds of billions of dollars of our money, money we'll never see or be able to use to make our own lives better, and you'll know who these phony wars have been waged to benefit. You don't have to be Harry Houdini to figure it out.

There are a lot of co-tactics they can use as the basic big lies begin to wear thin and the public starts waking up. Our consciences are still intact, and the deaths of thousands of innocent people, much less over a million, for most of us is a horror beyond comprehension. People do finally begin to see that they've been lied to and used. Then they begin to complain and speak out. Almost every complaint has been anticipated and, as you've witnessed, when the complaints hit the fan, they are cast aside with a single message from the 'party' in control. Like mockingbirds they all repeat the same sentences. They all make the same bogus claims. They try to turn it around and make the truth out to be a lie, and make the ones criticizing them out to be 'for the terrorists'. This is very dangerous stuff.

It goes further than that too, they've thought this through for a very long time. They knew how to take advantage of the publics emotions as soon as 9/11 happened and get us to connect whatever they were planning to do to security and safety. They knew their lies about going to war would slowly but surely break down as people became aware of the reality of what was being done, and they knew people would see right through the lies and claims that wars and brutality could in any way bring us peace of mind. It's an obvious oxymoron by itself. They also knew that in spite of their ready-to-go think tank created strategies to keep the public unbalanced and unable to confront the leadership to demand changes, after a while the numbers of people would grow large enough to finally be able to make them shut up and get real. They could only use tactics to attack and destroy critics for so long.

So, quietly in the background they built and refurbished prison camps right here, on our own soil, and the same big corporations who are raking it in Iraq got the no-bid contracts. They're even on retainer.

The police have systematically been turned into soldiers, not public servants. They are turned into violent thugs who are encouraged to see the public as the enemy and treat us with ever increasing brutality. The prisons are growing like wildfire, indeed they may be one of the only industries on American soil that are growing. This government intends to keep people from waking up, from catching on and from stopping them, no matter what it takes.

With continued total domination of the media that never allows a dissenting channel to come into mass view, they continue to spin their lies and control games and for those who dare to speak up they are ready with astonishing speed to have those people dragged away. This government is clearly terrified that at any moment the public will suddenly wake up and tear them from their liars thrones and give them what they so richly deserve.

Our descent into Orwell's world is well underway, it's not even a question of potential danger, we're in it. We're in it, when the government is standing up for it's own law breaking, standing up and arguing in defense of torture, standing up and claiming that corporations are people and that people are not people and so they deserve no due process. It happens when liars lie and mix two unrelated things to inspire our emotions to control our thoughts and actions. We will blindly follow them anywhere they lead us, even if it's right into hell.

Oh yes, it's a very slick, very well orchestrated operation this bush regime has going. It's been staffed with the world's greatest experts in propaganda techniques to keep Americans on board for as long as possible. Endless lies keep on coming while old lies are repeated and the ones that don't work are quickly discarded and not mentioned again. Many lies are interwoven too, to make layers of lies that are carefully catapulted out to the public to make us think and feel exactly what they want us to think and feel. All it takes is information control and repetition of the lies on every major news channel. People can only draw conclusions from the information available to them, so what they get in the way of information is very carefully decided and controlled. Yes, we have censorship in full swing, and propaganda to a degree so obvious to outsiders it makes their heads spin that we can't see it for what it is. But we can't see it.

The Layers Of Lies combined with Total Information Control makes it so much harder for our own people to extricate themselves from all of the deception. By and large the public will never be able to get a clear idea of who's who and what's really going on.

Most important of all are the foundational lies all the other lies are built on, and those continue to be repeated to this day. 'God and country.' 'Support the troops.' 'We're making progress.' 'Another 9/11 could happen any second unless you give up more of your rights.' The fear mongering, threats of dirty bombs, threats of home-grown terror, which is nonexistent, threats of raging pandemics, any threats at all that scare people and make them actually turn to the government and beg to be protected, those are the lies holding everything else up. As long as the public still believes the basic foundational lies, then whatever evidence comes up to prove that other sets of lies are indeed lies won't be enough to totally break through the deception and expose these guys for what they really are.

The tricks and tactics are getting more desperate too, they're breaking down every last one of our rights and tossing them aside to make sure we can't legally rise up against them. They've already halfway passed so-called anti-terror speech laws that entitle the government to imprison people who are aiding the terrorists just by criticizing the government. They're pushing hard to make dissenting opinions a death offense crime. That's desperation. They've made the foundational lies nearly untouchable through hyperpoliticization turning our congress into subservient lap dogs who are too afraid to speak the truth while the lies are still so widely believed. The bush regime will continue to get away with all of its crimes and wrongdoing as long as the public is kept in fear and anxiety suckling at the governments' big fat phony security teat, hysterically crying out to be kept safe from bogeymen.

They've got America right where they want America. Stupid, believing, and down on our knees begging them to make this country into a hellish police state, a nightmare of control and brutal tactics, a nation of sheep obedient to authority of any and all kinds, saying 'please' and 'thank you sir' to guys with badges. That's what the bush team knows it has to have in place long before the slowest Americans finally wake up and smell the coffee.

The bushco will continue to destroy our future as well as our present. It will continue giving our power to corporations, while it undermines us more and more, eventually leaving us under continual surveillance, bugged, DNA-sampled, drug-tested and reporting to authorities for every little thing. They are desperate to maintain total control and keep all of the ground they've gained through their lying and deceiving of the people.

Ground work is being laid through horrendous and shocking legislation that Congress just keeps on rubber-stamping. They've denied bush nothing, no matter how much damage it does to the people of this country. No matter how illegal his actions are, they stand by ready to make them legal and to cover for his partners in crime. They're injecting prisoners with animal tranquilizers, torturing people, jailing people without cause, without charges and without due process. They are snooping into every teeny space of our private lives to know what we're thinking so they can be prepared to knock us down, and we keep letting them do it, and we keep letting them get away with it.

Nixon famously said, "It's not a crime when the president does it." That pretty much tells you who these people are and how really willing they are to say anything it takes to keep people believing that they are good people who are working hard to protect this country. There does come a point, though, when only the most brainwashed are unable to see the wreckage piling up around all of us every single day. It's something I'd like to study. What does it take to wake some folks up when evidence up the yin-yang won't do it? Well, we're talking about the same animal here too. We're confronting emotion-based beliefs that came into being when liars lied and connected two things that have nothing in common so that they could get what they wanted from the trusting unsuspecting decent people standing before them.

I sincerely hope that bush's idea of Christianity is not an accurate take on Christian beliefs in the minds of American Christians. If it is, we're toast. In any case, we have to see how asserting religiosity is not proof of being a good person. We have to get it through our heads that church and state have no business being in bed together and that when they are, the offspring is hell spawn and death.

Thursday, February 14, 2008.

Non-Reality Theories

I think it's safe to say that most rational beings agree that facts and beliefs are not the same thing. Facts are statements of verified information, truths that are proven. Belief is choosing to decide that something is true in the absence of proof. Beliefs are not facts.

No matter how strongly or widely beliefs are held, a non-fact will not become a fact. Intensity of belief also has no effect on facts. Nor does it matter that a majority holds those beliefs, and even holds them with great intensity. Consensus, majority agreement, even intense agreement does not make reality, it just makes agreement.

If we are in agreement on those facts, then let's dive into the reality of non-reality theories.

Group Think

I've noticed that there is often a direct relationship between the number of people who share a belief and their aggregate inability to perceive the difference between fact and non-fact. The higher the number or more powerful the group is, the less likely they are to remember or care that there is a difference. For these it seems a 'majority rules' mindset is in place, resulting in the attitude that because they outnumber you or have more power than you, their non-facts are elevated to facts.

That's not possible, of course. Their non-facts will remain non-facts, because they are non-facts, regardless of taking a vote. It's called reality, and it may be inconvenient, but there it is anyway. As simple a fact as that is to grasp, as obvious and clear as it may be, it's astonishing how regularly it is ignored.

Sometimes facts are too contrary to our existing beliefs for us to be able to accept them. They may be facts we just don't like, but unfortunately, even if we hate them, it won't make them go away.

Opinions, feelings and beliefs have no effect on facts.

Reality is just not optional, even when large numbers of people choose to believe that it is.

Situations like that can quickly become scary and destructive because the fact is, you've got a whole group of people being dishonest with themselves who dislike the truth almost as much as those who speak it. The last thing they will tolerate hearing is any pesky evidence against their unprovable beliefs.

People swept away in self-deception have disconnected from the rules of fair and basic moral conduct. They will resist attempts to correct their disconnect, and no amount of facts or hard evidence will bring on correction. I think it's true to say that they have lost touch with reality, because very often they truly believe their disconnection from reality is the definition of reality.

When this situation exists in a large or powerful group, it will lead to harm. That is a given.

When people stop acting based on facts and reality, they will not achieve their desired outcomes, not ethically and not without extraordinary force, it's impossible. In order to achieve a desired outcome, we all have to work with the specific facts of the situation and stay in reality to get there.

It's a lot like baking a cake or building a motor. You need the correct ingredients or parts combined and constructed in the required order or you won't get a cake or a running motor.

There is really no way around this, and for those who insist there is, a long string of clashes, failures and harm is all that will ever come of their effort.

What's amazing is that they'll never concede that their failure to work with facts and reality is what's keeping them from getting what they want so badly.

Intelligence is Not a Factor

When, for whatever reason, individuals or groups take the leap out of known facts and reality, they embrace an alternate theory either of their own design or of pre-constructed design by others and then simply assert that their theory will work. These can be highly intelligent people and still fall victim to believing all kinds of unrealistic theories, and I think this is largely due to two things.

One is that theories that are not reality based can assert things as facts that are not facts and do so in a manner that seems to be reasonable. But reasonable is not factual; if they were the same thing, we wouldn't have two different words for them in the dictionary. Something may seem reasonable, but that doesn't make it factual. Not being able to tell what sounds good from what is real is an excellent way to screw yourself up.

The other thing at play boils down to fear. It's about wanting something that you can't get in reality, and often that's because what you want doesn't exist. But as much as we don't like to admit it, we humans are driven by our emotions and desires, and when we desire something badly enough, we are often willing to do almost anything to get it. That includes lying, cheating, stealing, killing and buying into non-reality theories and pretending they are better than reality. And the more we desire something, the less willing we are to release whatever theory it is that we perceive to be our only route to getting what we desire.

Experts

Our desire to believe is very strong, especially if what we are being given to believe speaks to our fears and promises to relieve them. We hate being uncertain and insecure, sometimes to the point of hysterics. I'm not sure why folks don't understand that life is very uncertain and insecure and there's really only so much we can do about that. If we take common sense precautions and don't do stupid things, we'll be as safe as you can possibly make yourself. But that fact is so unpleasant for many people that they want more than that, so they flock to the experts for advice. They've rarely, if ever, considered certain realities about experts that are rather obvious and very important.

Experts are the single most demonstrated group throughout history to be consistently proven dead wrong.

Experts are wrong about almost everything, if you think about it. All it takes is for a little time to pass, and the things popular experts were absolutely certain about ten years ago or a hundred years ago are not what they're saying today. The expert advice from yesterday never lives very long and is always, always changed to something else and forgotten about a little way down the road. Do you believe that in fifty years from now experts will be saying the same things they are saying today about medicine or science or any other field that has experts? It just won't happen. In fifty years from now they'll be talking about things we've never even heard of today.

In the first half of the 20th century medical experts got on television and told Americans that smoking cigarettes was good for you. In the last half of the century they were going on television saying that smoking cigarettes is bad for you.

Around the time of the Civil War experts scoffed at the idea that surgeons should clean their instruments or even wash their hands between patients. They found it ridiculous to think there were tiny little invisible things crawling around on their knives and fingers. The fact that some 90 per cent of patients survived surgery, but then went downhill and died within a few days was a mystery they could not explain, but they were experts, and they said it was nonsense that cleaning anything had a thing to do with it.

Experts and officials told us after dropping the bomb on Japan that there was no radiation and it was safe. Today experts are telling us that eating chemicals in our food is safe, and that vaccines are safe, and that GMOs are safe, and they aren't even providing data to back those things up. But people are so conditioned and so convinced that experts know everything, that many are suffering the consequences all around us and nobody can put two and two together. It's just not that hard to do, if you step back and look at the facts. It is very hard to do, if you simply choose to believe.

No matter what experts say, they can tell you about test results and data and charts and graphs, and it may sound very compelling and believable, but that doesn't make it true.

Experts are not necessarily people who know the truth. They are people who absorb and accept mass quantities of the current prevailing opinions and beliefs and mix them in with truths. Since opinions and beliefs are not facts, and consensus on beliefs does not make them facts, then, frankly, anyone who goes to experts to make their decisions for them risks making themselves into guinea pigs. They will become the basis for the data on the next new thing that experts believe in and present their data for.

Experts can also be liars. For the right amount of money or to achieve a little fame and prestige, you might really be surprised to find out how many times experts have looked you right in the eye and lied their asses off. And that's not a theory, that's a fact.

Statistics are definitely not facts, and if you've ever done the slightest bit of data gathering and crunching, you'll quickly see that results of any kind can be achieved by using whatever numbers you want to use. Unless you're willing to ask for the data used for any given statistics and then analyze them yourself, you have no idea what you're being given. It is virtually guaranteed, if an unrelated group were to gather statistics on the very same data, that the results would be different, sometimes profoundly different.

Being quick to believe non-facts in the real world is how we become victims time and again.

Harming Others is Bad

There is a time when allowing people with non-reality theories to proceed as desired is absolutely the wrong thing to do, and that is when the harm being caused is being done to others who want nothing to do with these people or their theories. When that's happening, I think, it prevails on all of us to speak up, even when we're outnumbered by non-reality theorists, and it's important that as many of us speak up as possible. Because at times like these there is often no stopping these folks from perpetrating great harm on a great many people unless we can surround them and outnumber them ourselves and force them to cease and desist. Hopefully peacefully.

Once major non-reality theories are underway, the folks behind it will have theorized every step they will take and every outcome of every action, and to whatever extent they have ignored facts and reality in any of those steps, they will fail. That failure will always surprise them too, but it will rarely illuminate them. They will simply dig in harder with even more non-reality-based theories until they are literally winging it and making it up as they go, often leaving a trail of destruction and serious harm in their wake.

These are people operating on belief, not on facts, and to say they are dangerous at this point would be an understatement.

I don't know why groups who share non-reality theories do this so very often, but they do. They do it in science, in medicine, in religious organizations, in law, pop culture, media, love and politics, and they hurt people every single time. Then to add insult to those they've injured, they blame their victims and indeed are often unwilling to admit that victims exist, because victims are proof that their theories are wrong.

I guess, when you're not dealing in facts, then you can make up the rules as you go, and you can even believe them. It's absolutely amazing how intricate these theories can become, and this is inevitable over time, because for every failure or unexpected bad result they must use more reasonable-sounding non-reality theory to explain away those failures. They will seem to have a fast answer for everything, a quick dismissal of every presented fact, and an absolute disinterest in hearing anything that overwhelmingly proves that they are wrong.

Again, this will not replace reality by even a single atom. This is true even when the stated goals are noble, or beautiful, or they have their hearts in the right places. That is all irrelevant. It is also irrelevant that they believe strongly, even with all of their being, that they can get what they so badly want through a non-reality theory. They will not be able to achieve it. It's so simple, it's almost confusing.

Something else I've noticed as I've watched these sorts of things play out on the world stage is that the more unreal the theories get the more dangerous these people tend to become. They often don't recognize that they are endangering others, and when others are hurt by their direct actions, they will deny it. When it can no longer be denied that others are being harmed by their actions, they will simply say outright that others being hurt is a price that must be paid in the glorious work they are doing for their good cause. This is the single most blatant evidence that they are working through non-reality theories. It's really up to those others getting hurt whether or not they are willing to sacrifice themselves in the name of any cause, and generally speaking, they aren't.

Instant self-excusing of any heinous or callous act is an inevitable part of this non-reality process, and at that point not taking a stand against it is helping them to perpetrate destruction and harm on others. Remember, the harm is all for nothing, because they cannot get where they want to go. It's all for nothing. They will wreak such profound damage and suffering on others that the carnage is beyond comprehension. Their disconnection from reality allows them to see that incomprehensible carnage as acceptable and justified in order to get what they want. If that's not the definition of insanity, then give me a better one.

Force and Head Games

Another tier of this non-reality theory system is that it will evolve into a situation where the believers begin to encounter so much dissent and disgust that the only way they can ensure they are able to continue doing things their unrealistic way is to use force. They must bludgeon their way forward after a certain point, and, ironically, when this point comes, they will begin to cry foul. They will begin to assert their 'right' to have their unreality theory and will assert their 'right' to harm as many others as they see fit in order to keep trying to alchemize non-reality into reality.

They have become so immersed in their belief system that to them reality is literally their enemy. Approaching them with facts and proof and evidence enrages them, and they will say that they are being persecuted for their beliefs, or that they are being unfairly denied their right to live their lives as they see fit. They will also completely miss the obvious fact that those they are harming also have rights. Usually, to them others do not have rights, only they do, and that's 100 per cent wrong. Everybody has the same human rights at all times and saying others don't is a hypocritical lie.

In official structures of this kind authorities will arrogantly assert as fact the obvious non-fact that because they are self-proclaimed experts or authorities they are right. As illogical as that is, they use it every day, and it works on the vast majority of people. In essence, they are demanding that entire subjects belong to them and only they may offer opinions on it and outside opinions by definition can be rejected out of hand.

Outside opinions and disagreement from within or without are perceived as a form of attack that hurls them into vindictive self-defensive arrogance, and anything remotely resembling a fact or reality will be long out of the picture. Regardless of the group or individual, they will claim a great many things that will accuse everyone else of working against them and seeking to destroy them.

They would be right about that in a way. If they've managed to enrage and offend enough outsiders to their group, it may very well be that those outsiders want to take revenge. But by and large that's not the goal. The goal is only to force them to stop, because what they're doing is invalid and causing irreversible and serious damage to innocent people or property or the environment or to society.

At this stage, specific non-reality mind games ramp up, and the poison of determined non-reality believers is nothing if not sticky. When they've realized that they no longer have support from outside, they will understand that their theory is under threat, and when that's apparent, they will use it as an excuse to defend themselves.

This is a critical moment that we have to understand exists, and we must be prepared for it. If we're unaware of this mind flip, this turning inside out of reality, we can easily be sucked into unreality and suddenly find ourselves unable to stand up to these people. What happens here is subtle but monstrous, it's clever but it's a false argument that goes like this. We say: "Your beliefs are not reality and your actions are hurting people. You may not continue doing those things. You must stop now." They respond: "You are being disrespectful of our beliefs. You hate us.

You want to kill us. We have the right to exist. We will not stop working toward our desired outcome. You are evil for attacking us." Or: "We are experts (or officials, or authorities) who know everything, and you are ignorant and know nothing. We have consensus, and that makes us right and you wrong. We can force you to accept our assertions, and your refusal to comply makes you an enemy (or a threat, or an incompetent, etc.)."

They are turning non-facts around and doing what got them there in the first place, which is to use reasonable-sounding assertions to justify their refusal to stop harming others. They are trying to turn attention back to us and put us on the defensive by asserting lies as facts and making some very serious, but very false accusations. Next they will claim they are forced to harm others in order to do the right thing, and if we try to stop them, it will prove them right.

It's easy to get hung up here, because it twists reason into a balloon animal that floats away before you can get a hold of it.

If we get trapped by reasonable-sounding assertions instead of staying firmly in facts, then they will prevail. As many people are quite reasonable, this trap is possibly one of the most dangerous and most difficult to expose. Worse, once people are trapped, they will also find it difficult to turn back. We need to recognize the ploy and call it for what it is.

In the above argument we stated facts and told them they are not justified to continue pursuing their goals in the present manner, because they are hurting innocent people. Their responses completely ignore the facts we just stated. They took off in completely unrelated directions that are of no interest to us, have no bearing on the situation or no basis in fact. They're attempting to turn blame away from themselves and onto us hoping to escape responsibility for their actions. They've sidestepped the subject, and we should have expected that. After all, it's the very reason we're all here in the first place. They are not functioning in reality, and it's hurting people.

We need to respond with facts. Whether or not we respect anyone's beliefs is irrelevant. Our private feelings for others are also irrelevant. Accusations that we want to kill anyone had best be made with solid proof to back them up, and proof should be immediately demanded. If they cannot supply it now, then they cannot make unsupported accusations now, and we must force that point to the top of the argument. Of course, proof never exists, because they are lying, and we can then say we recognize the ploy and insist that they face the charges and evidence against them. And last but not least, opinions are not facts.

Our response to their statements of non-reality should be: "What we are saying has nothing to do with your beliefs or anyone's feelings. What we are saying is that regardless of intent or beliefs or feelings, and regardless of your authority status, your actions are hurting others and they must stop now."

"Your actions are hurting others and they must stop now." That is what must be repeated, and all of their assertions that do not directly and factually respond to that statement *must be ignored*. This is the only field we came to play on, and we can't allow ourselves to be dragged off of it.

An example of asserting non-facts as if they were a given is in the infamous question, "So, how long have you been beating your wife Mr. Jones?"

The question asserts as fact that Mr. Jones beats his wife. The thing is Mr. Jones does not beat his wife and never has. But once this false assertion is made, it's a form of attack so underhanded and damaging that it can literally ruin Mr. Jones' life. The nature of the accusation, even though it's completely unfounded, stated as fact without any supporting evidence, is specifically intended to arouse strong emotions from anyone listening, which will result in people not caring about supporting facts or evidence. They will simply hate Mr. Jones.

This is the same strategy used by major media to strongly sway public opinion away from a true guilty party like a huge corporation or even the government and actually turn the victims into something so scary-sounding and ugly that people emotionally react with fear and loathing. No one offers or asks for evidence to support assertions that the accused really are in a cult, or really is a child molester, or is a terrorist mastermind, or any other ugly accusation. It works too. It works every time.

It's truly that easy to get people sucked into non-reality theories by the millions. It happens every single day, and very few people are aware that the game even exists. We usually have no idea to what extent we're operating on a set of completely false beliefs and we would deny that to be the case. Of course we will deny it without checking any facts, because we've fully bought into the knee jerk emotional reaction, so you can see how insidious and difficult to solve this problem can be.

I can't help but wonder about the fact that most of us know very little about the most common types of lies and deceptions. Why don't we? Could it be that those in powerful places use lies so often and to such great advantage that the subject of lies is purposely never brought up in public discourse? If we were all quick to recognize typical kinds of big fat lies, it would be very difficult for others to manipulate us into beliefs that are absolutely wrong, yet quickly become unshakable. It would be a great advantage to those who understand the game, but for those who do not even know the game exists, there would be little to keep them from being driven to the desired responses like sheep.

These and many other similar scenarios are based on the same thing – non-reality theories that are perpetrated due to the fact that as a society we have the unfortunate habit of allowing groups with harmful beliefs to act in unreasonable ways. Unfortunately, once any non-reality theory becomes systemic, it is incredibly difficult to clean it up. It can take a century of dedicated effort by many people who don't even know each other who are willing to go against the status quo and keep repeating the facts, which can be a very dangerous thing to do. Many who have done so throughout history and today ended up deprived of justice, freedom, life or limb, because non-reality theorists usually become quite brutal in the face of dissent.

Recognizing the many kinds of non-reality theories around us today is a good skill to develop if we are at all interested in knowing the truth about our world and our lives and if the idea of being manipulated by unknown others bothers us. We can't hope to know the score if we don't even realize there's a game going on. And there always is a game going on.

I believe that everyone deserves to be treated respectfully unless they prove otherwise, so learning to be diplomatic and allowing others to have their take on things, even if they are clearly non-reality-based is something we are obligated to do for one another. After all, to them, reality is non-reality, and we don't want to be incendiary, hopefully. If their non-reality theory does not involve us or affect us, then there is no basis in claiming it's any of our business what they believe. Using humor is also a good tool, and if push comes to shove and you are overruled and outnumbered, I personally couldn't blame you for saying whatever they want to hear, if it means getting out of that situation in one piece. That's not dishonesty, it's playing by the same rules they are. When in Rome, you know what I mean?

We have our work cut out for us along these lines today, I'm afraid, because non-reality theory has taken hold of the steering wheel on all of the biggest buses. We're being driven to the edge by people who think they're gracing us with their disconnection from the truth, and that's about as dangerous as it gets. I don't know what can be done to change it, usually all we can change is ourselves. Surviving it may be the best we can hope for as this growing storm continues to darken the skies above us.

There are some times we cannot do anything but take cover, and that's a survival skill also worth having. Just gaining the ability to recognize the difference between facts and beliefs will be of very good use in any case and will help us decide how to best handle the serious challenges we're facing now and will continue to face no doubt for the rest of our days. And that's a fact.

Tuesday, March 4, 2008.

Interference

I'm looking around me today and seeing people and hearing the great wash of talk. Everyone is talking past each other and not even trying to connect. The country has been shattered and then coalesced back not into one loose knit organism, but into fragmented groups who can't see anything eye to eye. The groups have all staked out their own territory and regardless of the inner message of the group the outer message is basically some variation of, "You're with us or you're against us."

Gee. I wonder where that came from… Well, I don't really wonder at all, I think we all know where that came from. It was a message that circled the world in a day some few years ago and who'd have ever guessed it would have changed everything? But it sure did change everything. It ruined everything. It ruined the unity we had, replacing it with disunity, which is of course very unpleasant. Then they told us, "You need your unity back, come let us bomb our way to unity." They just wanted their own kind of unity. They had to destroy the kind we already had first. Those seven little words did a lot to accomplish that.

"You're with us or you're against us."

That one simple sentence set the precedent and the foundation for the world to enter into endless disunity, an endless disunity only they could fix. It's a message that provoked, that separated, that insulted and that interfered with freedom on every conceivable level. It's a message that is presumptuous and sounds like nails on a blackboard to many and like sweet-sweet music to a small number of others.

To the die-hard followers of America it sounded like the ultimate leadership symphony of their unfulfilled dreams had finally been written. To the hard-core self-superior militants of America it sounded like the music of their hearts desire, the march to victory.

The much longed for oh-come-ye symphony of the followers has always been a lot like Atlantis, being that it was a thrilling theory, but did not exist in reality. At least not until those words were spoken. The followers found nirvana in those seven little words spoken by a leader who to them emanated everything they'd been aching for since the misdeeds of 1776.

Here was a man who cared not for the thoughts, feelings, opinions or very real needs of others. He was all about himself and he said, "Screw everybody else. I want what I want and I'm taking it." To the followers that meant he had the strength of his convictions, and whether or not those convictions were actually comprised of any virtue, didn't matter. They wanted someone unwavering to follow and at long last they found him. They are still intoxicated by his 'strength', long after most who initially embraced the man have rejected him and his contentious, small-minded hypocritical brutal style. At least someone is happy around here. What's that old saying? Oh yes. Ignorance is bliss.

And the hard-core self-superior militants were thrilled to bursting with those seven little words spoken with all of the hubris they so longed to hear. Their hungry dream had come into reality, and who couldn't appreciate the high of having your dream come true? They were on high, because they would finally be totally free to approach the world with their one and only tool, an enormous gleaming and sooty hammer. No matter what problem arose on planet Earth, the militants could now grab their hammer and yell, "Geronimo!" – and descend to places far and wide where they'd appear with smiles, teeth gleaming in the daybreak. "Here I come to save the day!" is their theme song, and they assume it's everybody's favorite song. In fact, they insist on it, or rather, their leader insists on it.

It isn't everybody's favorite song, of course, but it turns out if anyone admits that, they get the hammer. So, we've all learned the words and the melody, and even if it chokes us, we'll hum along, or lip sync, at least as long as they're looking. And while we're finding it impossible to endure even one more note of that malodorous refrain, the militants are still swinging their hammer, and swinging their hammer, and swinging their hammer.

Surely, if they were using it properly they'd have built something by now. Surely, we should see a breathtaking new city across the ocean, rising high above the din, inspiring awe in all who behold it. Surely, there would be such an amazing new thing so beautiful and so filled with truth as to cause all hearts to swell and eyes to moisten around the world for all who see it; instead of endless acres of rubble and smoke and broken things and broken bodies. Surely. Zeus knows we've paid for it. My God, have we paid for it.

But the hammer does not build, it only destroys what it touches. I wish they'd consider adding more tools to their tool kit, but they do seem to be absolutely enamored of their hammer. The multitrillion dollar hammer that only destroys.

The biggest chunk of our shared wealth goes to aid the pounding into dust of people and places far away. They aren't singing songs about us. They aren't greeting us with flowers. They'd like us to stop pounding them now, please, they've been saying so for years. Our reply? "Nonsense! Here we come to save the day, and everybody wants their day saved! Carry on! Sally forth! Chin up! There is much yet to accomplish! We shall not leave until the whole place is in ruins!"

It's a bit like burning down the house to get rid of mice, only it's a hell of a lot more expensive. And destructive. And ultimately it's become sickening to the soul of the world, which is bent over puking its guts out.

Sigh.

Whatever happened to listening? Do we not all have ears? I know we do. We are listening. The problem is what we are listening to. The voice. The solo voice that is coming out of the mouths of the only people who have access to the major streams of information broadcasting in the country. They're all the same damn voice. They look different, they have different hair and different genders, but when they open their mouths, it's as though they're channeling the same spirit from beyond.

Could it be they're all possessed? Do we need to hold a gigantic national exorcism? We'll be up to our fannies in pea soup if that's the case, because this is one powerful, pervasive spirit. Unfortunately, it seems to have also possessed a major avenue of having it exorcised. The church has also come under its spell. They too are showing all of the signs: the spinning heads, the speaking strange words that defy decency, the dark pleasure of offending onlookers. The arrogance. The depraved indifference to the innocent, the blindness to and dismissal of the truth. They've become the willing partners of the dark force and no longer seem able to notice how much they've changed into something frightening to behold.

We do have a problem on our hands. I have no idea how to exorcise an entire nation of it's demon. It may just be that it has to wear itself out after a ravenous glut spanning decades, after its blood feast and subsequent defecation, after changing our golden panorama into a barren dung heaped prairie that will take four million years to stop being radioactive before we can send in the pooper scoopers. Say, that would be a good job for the militants. They should honestly be charged with some of their own clean-up, it's only fair. But all they've got is their hammer. They can't scoop poop with a hammer.

Oh, trouble and worry and strife. Frustration and stupidity and zeal. We never run out of those things, they're abundant. Why on earth haven't the hot-rod kings of free money for the rich figured out a way to get those commodities on the markets? Maybe it's because those are the things they leave in their trail of exhaust as they zoom by, leaving our clothing in shreds and our hair tied in impossible knots. Thanks, financiers. How can we ever repay you? We'd like to, believe me, we'd really like to.

It seems like this teeming sea of individuals we call America cannot find center and focus, each one, one at a time, and then once more all together again. No one remembers that if we wanted to we could look at one another and say, "I disagree with every single word you just said, but I'd fight to the death for your right to say them." We find the idea of those words revolting. We've totally forgotten what freedom means.

We no longer care about making a welcoming world where everyone can be who they are and not have to endure relentless attacks based on the inescapable reality that we are not all the same and never can be. It's not a problem, it's just plain old reality. It's the way things must be, the only way they can be. But now the groups are clamoring and contriving up ways to eliminate those of unlike mind.

What we need is some silence. A great shared moment of silence. A few weeks of nothing streaming into our heads from outside of our heads, intruding, always unasked for, always full of content we never pre-approved. A couple of months, or better yet years, to allow our own thoughts to form and take shape again, to guide ourselves again from within, each one, one by one, regaining ownership and control of our own unique being.

But it's too noisy to concentrate. It's too busy to find a peaceful place to sit down and sink into the mossy bank of a sweet-smelling freshwater stream, to inhale the musky smell of nature and exhale the cares of the silly ass world. I think we need to do that, and I think we'd be a lot more likely to do it if it weren't for all that damned interference. Those outer signals demanding our full attention. Absorbing our entire mental output. Forcing us along whether we want to go along or not.

It's unnatural, you know. Our thoughts are supposed to be self-generated. That's why we each have our own head. We are not the Borg. Let me restate that, we are not supposed to be the Borg. The idea of mass conformity should repel us in no uncertain terms. We're supposed to question authority, question everything, and refuse to comply with stupidity for the simple reason we don't have to. We're supposed to laugh at foolish men, not reward them with our loyalty. We're supposed to have enough sense to know right from wrong and care about the difference. It's not like we need to be told what they are, we know. At least we should know. But the voice, the interference, that nonstop droning on that is quickly redefining the country, that is turning it inside out and upside down, that is sucking the life out of us, draining us of prosperity and good will, that voice will not shut up. All day. Every single day. Every moment of every day of our lives, that voice drones on and on. Demanding. Lying. Hating. Undermining. Interfering. It's stealing America, one mind at a time.

Like a great floating invisible spider it injects it's numbing poison under the skin, paralyzing the brain so that it can no longer feel or generate a response. Then it feeds. It sucks the brains out and gulps them down then fills the cavity with that voice. It says, "This is up!" – and then presses the down button, and nobody notices.

A few do notice. And they are quickly branded dissident, loony, crazy. Yes, I'm crazy. I can see with my own two eyes and hear with my own two ears and think with my own personal brain, which is not hooked into the central core computer. It rejects the voice, physically. The voice makes me ill, literally. I know that voice is the voice of death. If they stopped calling me names, I'd know something was wrong, the last thing I want is their doting admiration. I want to offend them, they deserve it. I want to shock them back into reality. I want them to find their own center and disconnect from the hive core, to stop taking its orders, to start breathing again, to start seeing again, to start loving the world and everyone and everything in it again.

I don't want much, do I? I just want to live in a world where people recognize there's nothing that hard about being decent to one another. There's enough to go around. There's no need to tear anyone to shreds. We can handle the differences, they really aren't all that different. We will always have so much more in common than not, but all we can see anymore are those differences, those things that add the spice and variety that makes it all so worthwhile. Now we see those differences as a threat. They are a threat, to the hive. To the drive for conformity. To the desire to create a bland sea of all-the-same nodes, being compliant and obedient to the voice, bowing and curtsying on cue, until the steps are deeply memorized and no one ever disagrees. How that can be anybody's idea of perfection eludes me? How a nation who believes in freedom can embrace that does not make sense? But there it is anyway.

Damned interference. If we could only pull the plug. If we could pull the plug and experience the sudden end of the electronic signals, that amazing moment when all of the tension leaves the body and we're suddenly aware of how noisy it's all been. When the silence is immediately calming and delicious and we want to turn around and hug somebody and kiss them on the forehead and say, "What on earth got into me? Let's take a walk, shall we? It's a lovely day."

I want to pull the plug on all of that interference, but I can't do it for anyone but myself. Everyone will have to unplug themselves to grab their freedom back. I do believe it's the only way we'll ever get out of this nightmare. But is it too late? Do all of these people actually want to be plugged into the Borg core interface? Is 24 hour interference the new reality? Is interference the new normal? It truly frightens me to the bone. It just may be.

And I may be the last of a small dying breed, a group without a name, without a core, without a membership. The next endangered species that nobody much cares about anyway. The good news is, when I'm gone, when all of those like me are gone, no one will grieve. No one will notice. No one will care. No one will even understand what I was or what I was talking about. They'd laugh and say, "My goodness, what an odd malformation of the hive. It happens. There's no comprehending it, it's better that they're all gone. Silly creatures with their nonsensical babble. They sounded so foolish. Too stupid to recognize how ridiculous they were. It's best they're gone."

Indeed. The age of the hive is upon us. All hail interference. Either that or go get yourself some earplugs.

Saturday, March 8, 2008.

The First Corporation

Thousands of years ago people lived in close-knit clans and the population of the world was only a tiny fraction of what it is now. People could go an entire life time without ever encountering a stranger. Unfortunately, sometimes strangers purposely encountered them.

One particular day at one particular village a very long time ago such an encounter took place. It was just after dawn on a foggy morning that the village clan was going about its normal morning routine. Firewood was gathered, fires were lit, and food preparation was underway. Mothers breast-fed their babies, children played, and elders sat waiting to be fed.

The comforting sounds of fire crackling and children laughing were interrupted by the muffled rumbling of hoof beats and the sharp clatter of scraping metal coming from somewhere beyond the fog. The sounds grew louder and more distinct by the second, and so, sensing danger, the people of the clan quickly gathered together in the center of the camp. Moments later, emerging from the haze, came a terrifying vision: men on horseback draped in animal skins and headpieces with long pointed horns, their faces painted, some wearing masks with menacing non-human expressions. The villagers had never seen anything like this before. Not knowing if these beings were humans, spirits, or even monsters, their hearts thumped hard in their chests as they stood paralyzed, watching the creatures growing nearer.

As was intended, the strangers had caught the village inhabitants completely by surprise. They rode into the camp then viciously slew every man in the village with razor-sharp flesh-cutting blades. Throats were slashed and skulls were crushed; innocent blood flowed in hot rivers and soaked the ground. Violence like this had never been seen there before.

The women and children were shocked and traumatized, and they tried to run, but they could not escape. They were all rounded up and brought back to the center of the camp, then separated into two groups, women on this side, and children on that side. Some of the horrifying creatures searched through every dwelling and looked up every tree to make certain they'd found every last member of the clan.

When all of the women and children had been found and separated, the strangers dismounted their horses and killed every child one by one. Babies, toddlers, everyone under the age of 12 was slain with swift deliberation. They then turned their attention to the women. Any who were old, sick, or pregnant were also killed. The rest would be taken to be their slaves and wives. They took whatever pillage they found desirable from the camp, then pulled the women onto their horses in front of them and began the journey home.

Behind them lay a sickening scene of incomprehensible carnage. Bloody, dismembered dead bodies of children, women and men were the last thing the surviving women saw before being dragged onto the horses and taken away. The innocent dead were the silent remnants of a story that no one would ever hear.

The brutal strangers whipped their horses with leather straps and rode them hard, desiring to get home before nightfall. They made good time and when they arrived they beat the women, raped some of them, humiliated them, and began to break them. Over the following days they forced them to cook and clean for them, sew their garments and make their living spaces comfortable. The women gathered wood, tended the fires, brought water for their households and slowly accepted the imposed routines of their new unasked for lives. They also wept for their murdered children and husbands and mothers and fathers and other family members, but they did so only when they would not be caught and punished for their tears. Within a year the women began giving birth to the children of their rapist captors.

Things being as they may, some of the women came to accept the men who took them as wives, but others were not so lucky. For the unlucky ones no love was in the man they lived with. No kindness existed in his heart, and no interest existed in him for her. He wanted progeny and he wanted a slave, and he got both through brutality and violence; not because brutality and violence were necessary, but because brutality and violence gave him total control.

These men, devoid of love or kindness, were single-minded and driven by a simple fact: they could exponentially increase their power and wealth through the use of organized mass murder carried out on defenseless people who were taken by surprise.

They perfected the art of this psychopathic behavior over the course of many years and countless attacks on villages and settlements none of which were ever prepared to defend themselves against the slaughter and brutality these men wrought. This became their stock in trade, and within two generations an entire ideology developed wherein the practitioners of organized mass murder deified and worshipped themselves and each other with the greatest respect going to the most brutal, most psychopathic and most murderous among them. These were the first CEOs, commonly referred to as kings. They deified themselves before the people to become the church, and the combination of king and church became the state.

The rest is history. It is also the present, for little has changed in the ways of men who to this day continue to profit through the mass slaughtering of innocents and the plundering of their lands.

Today it has become more sophisticated only in that they have been able to convince others to go and do the slaughtering for them and bring the plunder back to the CEOs. The weapons have evolved with the development of technology, but in the end they do the same as their earliest counterparts, they kill innocent people as quickly as they can be wielded. They kill more people with increasingly less effort every passing decade.

The expense of creating these modern weapons to stock the armed forces that use them is far beyond need or justification, because the CEOs long ago knew how to profit from that too. They own the vast enterprises that build the war camps and which manufacture and sell the weapons that are used to perpetrate the genocide and theft of resources all over the world. They don't fund a penny of it and they never have to get their own hands dirty. Their own lives are never in danger. It is all done for them, at no cost to them and at no risk to them whatsoever. It is we they convince to do their slaughter for them, pay for it all, and take every risk and loss unto ourselves.

Today's most powerful CEOs aren't much different from their earliest embodiment. They are no less dangerous. Their attire has changed from animal skins and fearsome masks to tailored suits and silk ties. No longer on horseback, they now ride in limousines to boardrooms and back rooms to claim their victories, engaging in brutal tactics that continue to decimate millions of lives in their endless drive for more wealth and more power.

Today they are able to walk among us unrecognized for they have mastered the fine arts of subterfuge and psychological manipulation to the point of gaining and maintaining total control over the minds of people everywhere.

Are they to be commended for their achievements? They would contend that their superior ability to kill, deceive and enslave mankind deserves high recognition, and that because of their brutality and dishonesty they are the superiors of all men. But today, just like thousands of years ago, they would be wrong to make such a claim, and they know that. That is why they dare not speak such things where others could hear them and recognize them for who and what they are. What they are is the greatest evolution of human evil this world has ever known. They embody and inspire every vile potential of mankind.

It takes no talent whatsoever, no thought, higher or otherwise, no particular intellect and no effort to be driven by greed and lusts and to live without compassion for others. Blunt force murder is the failure of mankind, not its apex. The CEOs, the state, are deceiving themselves as much as they are deceiving this world. They are Earth's slow children, retarded in moral development, the most truly disabled among us, for these men have no souls and so they can never be whole. They would be pitiable, but the nature of their disease makes them singularly difficult to feel any pity for.

Forced Ideology is Total Control

The propaganda of war mongers has bled deeply into the fabric of our culture and has for hundreds of years been successfully used to bring citizens to their feet and willing to go off to fight their desired wars. The looting and plundering is the primary goal, the theft of the wealth of others. But this is never told to the people they lie into blind cooperation. Other stories are told, often complex and compelling stories that instill fear in the public. Fear is the primary motivating tool behind war, the most effective tool in the propaganda arsenal.

Depictions of foreign strangers as monstrous enemies with inhuman traits and offensive belief systems are the meat of the feast of successful war propaganda, and no substantial evidence to support the claims of imminent doom is asked for or provided. The claims usually defy logic and facts, but are crafted with such great expertise, the tellers are able to mix opposing ideas into good-sounding excuses for war. The Holy War is an example of this mixing of opposites, and patriotism is a concept used to manipulate the emotions of the masses. Propaganda is profoundly effective, and that is why it is the first step to waging any war. Without it, there would be no chance that people anywhere would be moved to kill anyone.

If you doubt that modern wars are fought for the purpose of gaining wealth and power for the few at the expense of the many, then answer these questions. Why is war the most profitable business there is? Why isn't profiting from war held in utter disregard? Why isn't it illegal? If the reasons for war are so very pure and noble, then why do the same ranks of individuals always become so incredibly wealthy war after war after war? If there was not a penny to be made in war, would we still go off to fight them?

It is after all you and I who pay for war with our money and our lives. Our hard-earned dollars are directly transferred from our pockets to the pockets of wealthy men with our government serving as the enforcing agent. We have no choice but to pay. It is the high level officials who call for war and who more and more are the very same men who head up the major corporate entities, including the corporate media that profit so abundantly from war. Take the money away, take the profits away, take the media's relentless war propagandizing away, make war profiteering illegal and reduce profits from war to mere pennies, and just see how much war would be waged.

The greed and brutality of a small class of people make up the foundation the rest of society is built on. They are always at the top, and we are always at the bottom. They are always in the position to make and enforce all of the rules, and we are not allowed to break them. They take our money at gunpoint and we are not allowed to refuse to fund their endless capital ventures. We do all of the work, pay for everything, they get rich, and we get a paycheck that is only a bare fraction of our fair share of the wealth we create. They keep it. And they keep taking more, getting stronger, and we keep losing our just share of power, wealth and prosperity.

Unless and until we can see this, it will continue. It will keep getting worse and we will keep suffering as they keep gaining what they so endlessly desire. All of the money, all of the power, all of the control over all of us, that is, those of us they decide to let live.

A Different World

Without these violent greedy war mongers deciding our fates, we could have a completely different world. If it were up to us to determine our own fate, to design our own world and future, would we do it as they have? Would we poison our own air and water and destroy our own environments?

Would we have so much need for money, when the fact is that our birthright on this earth includes our entitlement to take whatever we need for our lives from earth's abundant natural resources? We don't have to destroy it to use it. We know perfectly well that destroying our world is suicide.

There is no justifiable reason and no need for a small group of men to lay claim to and hoard the massive natural wealth that belongs to everybody, including future generations. There is no right for those who are obsessed with greed and control to deprive us and coming generations of our birthright, our share of a pristine healthy natural environment that we all need to sustain our lives; or to preempt our ability to prosper and justly participate in the shaping of our society and our own private lives.

The combination of arrogant indifference to others, limitless greed and the use of overpowering violence is the most serious underlying disease of mankind.

Sadly, even today there is no known cure for this cancerous disease of the mind and soul. Other than forcing strict constraints and strong regulations on those infected and watching them like hawks every moment of the day, there is little we can do to prevent their addictive penchant for death and destruction. That is, unless we finally as a whole wake up to the simple reality that we've all been deprived of our rightful lives, our rightful chance to experience our own potential, and to define that potential for ourselves. We are captive and bound by laws that force us to comply with the desires of the greedy and the violent. The propaganda they spew keeps our minds entrapped. Freeing ourselves from their relentless tactics and strategies that seek to frame our thoughts for us is essential. Our thoughts must be our own, or we will remain entrapped forever.

A world of peace, prosperity and plenty could exist without the dark, powerful influences and manipulations of greedy, violent men, and that thing we mindlessly refer to as war would never have come into existence without them. They would have us thank them for that as if it were some great gift to the world. It is not a gift, it is the greatest curse that ever was. The recognition they truly deserve, should it ever come, will not be gratitude. It will take the form of full exposure to the public of their deceit, betrayal, manipulation and unfettered disdain for mankind. It would be their complete undoing.

But that time will never come on its own, nor will it come by force. It can only come about because we the people have changed ourselves, changed the way we see the world, literally changed our old ways and habits that lead us into mindless conformity and unwavering support for people and systems that exist only to undermine us and cheat us, even to kill us. It will come, when we individually disconnect ourselves from the raging rivers of propaganda and the many and various glittering cult stars and personalities who talk up thundering storms about freedom while in fact they are working to deprive us of that freedom and are doing so right before our unseeing eyes. It is we who have to wise up to bring the insanity to an end. We cannot change them and we cannot hope to change the systems that control our lives unless we change ourselves first.

We must regain the ability to see ourselves as worthy and deserving of full equity with the wealthy self-promoting cannibalistic classes that see us as lesser beings. To the extent we accept their judgments of us is the extent that we will continue to live life on our knees and on their selfish terms. We are their equals, and they are not above any one of us. They are no wiser, no better, and no more deserving than the least of us. There should not even be a 'least of us'. That we cannot understand that speaks to the depth of our own brainwashing and the acceptance of the value systems that deprive us of what is our rightful fair share of everything life has to offer.

When we hold the clear knowledge that power, greed and the desire to control others is the eternal ongoing battle that always has and continues to define our world, profoundly affecting everything and everyone in it, then we can hope to bring about the changes we need. When we all comprehend that this power struggle will never end, that the desire to bring about systems that give the few all of the wealth and power at the expense of everyone else will never go away, only then can we hope to bring a genuine end to the repeating foundational theme of self-destruction on which everything else is built. The wars, injustice and suffering that keeps our country stuck in self-defeating systems of mass belief, mass consumption and mass indifference to the truth are the product of our refusal to see ourselves and the systems that control us for what they really are.

Since that first attack on horseback to slaughter and control others the world has never been free, and it is not free now. We believe we are free, but we are not and never were. Our ignorance of everything real and factual keeps us believing something that simply is not true. We are more tightly controlled than ever and that control is becoming ever more brutal. Our choices are dwindling and the system itself is becoming impenetrable, making itself our eternal master. The system seeks only to protect and perpetuate itself, it is not interested in freedom or justice, and if you simply break any of their rules, even the most unjust of them, you'll quickly find that out. Freedom will not come until the corporate/state monopoly of control and the artifice of righteous violence in the name of good is understood and finally rejected. That is what is meant by "Knowledge is Power". Our knowledge of the truth is what will reduce the corrupt controllers to irrelevance, powerlessness and shame.

It is a choice. We can choose to know the truth, and once we know the truth, we must live it and speak it. We must rock the boat in order to break free of the powerful grip of false beliefs that control the majority of our minds. We must be willing to offend and disrupt in order to speak the truth, if that's what it takes. The truth must never be subordinate to disapproving opinions, which in themselves are a potent tool of social control. We must value real peace more than the instant gratification, the false peace that comes from choosing to conform specifically to avoid the necessary confrontations required to bring the truth back into public discourse. We must fearlessly, unapologetically question everything, question authority and demand justice for the least of us until there is no such thing as a least of us.

Our official overriding and controlling philosophy of depraved indifference, vengeful self-superiority and criminality is sheer evil, and the seed of that evil is something inside all of us. That must be recognized, and we must consciously choose to reject it. When we teach our children to recognize and to remember what true evil really is and where it really comes from, then and only then can we hope to make this a country that is honestly committed to making our highest principles a reality. A world of justice, peace and freedom will come about as soon as we start living in it. We can do that anytime. We can even do it now.

Monday, March 17, 2008.

Double Standards and Crazy Conspiracy Theorists

Very early in life we are all introduced to the concept of people who 'rule' over other people. At such a tender, innocent age, when mommy and daddy read us bedtime stories (do they still read bedtime stories?), we are each introduced to the idea of 'special' people who can tell us what to do and that we have to obey them.

Whether this stuff is read to children from storybooks or whether that exquisitely important parent to child interface is outsourced to a DVD player, things have not changed in hundreds of years. The implantation of that critically important notion before the age of reason is achieved with every single boy and girl on the planet. The youngest child will always know what a princess, a prince, a king and a queen are before they're six years old.

That permanent mental cement is poured and hardened before children can read or write for themselves, while they still need someone to cut their meat for them into tiny pieces, before their baby teeth grow all the way in, and for a great many children it will happen long before they are out of diapers. That foundational brain cement becomes, quite literally, a basic part of their mental foundation, forming their basic belief system about how the world works.

It's no surprise that no child is left behind when it comes to being introduced to the idea of certain people having rights of rulership over others. The storybook concept of certain people ruling over other people, so gentle and lovely, becomes a hard-core belief that is never questioned. It is foundational, so the idea of having someone who is in some way special and better than you, telling you what you can and can't do, or even ordering your death, or calling your nation to war, all seems perfectly normal. It would not seem normal at all without the foundational beliefs being laid at such a very young age across the board.

Whatever concepts are introduced to a child's growing brain are no trivial thing, although strangely, we have been led to think otherwise. We believe that since we don't remember our earliest years that there's nothing in there. As a consequence of that assumption, some people have sexual intercourse in the same room as their toddler, because they believe it won't register. Nor will the physical abuse register, daddy beating mommy black and blue, the drinking, swearing, shouting, the seething hatred and the tears. Little Jr. is believed to be too small to remember any of this nightmare. He won't remember crying for hours, cold and hungry and frightened. He won't remember that nobody picked him up and held him and caressed him, comforted him. He won't remember the sheer terror and panic he felt for what felt like forever. He's even too small to remember being yanked from his crib and hurled against the wall. Thank goodness, we say, that they don't remember these awful things when they get older.

I'm sorry, but they do remember them. Not in words perhaps, but in any of the diverse other ways the experiences of our lives are lived and stored. And where are they stored but in the physical structure of the brain. That's about as permanent a memory as there is.

Children's brains are in the most extraordinary state and rate of growth from birth to about five years old. Every thought, sensation, sight, sound, color, contrast, texture, emotion, feelings of hunger, cold and warmth, the smell of mother's body, dad's pipe, family dinners, the sounds of voices, music, machines, and weather, don't just pass through one ear and out the other. The brain captures every last one of them. Even the subconscious perceptions are registered, things beneath the conscious awareness.

The brain perceives it all and files it, beginning the process of building the unique central data base and operating system of that person. It is the most astronomical feat of data retention, cross-referencing and data retrieval in the known universe. This is the miraculous, living, real-time capacity of the human brain. It's an organic, thinking, feeling computer that responds and reacts, changes and grows, shrinks and dies off as we go about living our lives.

Pathways are established that are traveled again and again, but when there is something new, and everything is new the first five years of life, the brain literally grows its physical parts based on the data, sensations, thoughts, feelings, sights, sounds and smells of every single experience it perceives. And it all sticks. Forever. It's all a part of the foundation the entire rest of the brain and the person will be built upon.

In the same way that a house needs a good foundation, so does the human brain. And when that is lacking, the house may seem fine on the outside, but it will have some very precarious weaknesses and perhaps some strangeness in the general floor plans as well. When corners are cut such as the laying of a strong foundation, it's only logical to expect that other shortcuts were taken as well. Doors might open to reveal a brick wall. A room may exist with no floors. Lights might never come on or go off. Things tend to not be very stable on a poor foundation. It only takes a good hard push or two, which could be withstood by a well-built house, to shove an entire structure off its poor foundation.

Human beings seem much more able to cope with the scars, wounds and deficiencies that are a normal part of life, at least in its present evolution, than houses can. But injury is injury, damage is damage, and missing parts are missing parts. Pain and struggle are never totally forgotten. It all comes with us wherever we go, for the rest of our lives. It's a good reason to be a little nicer to each other, I think.

Considering how little thought we give and how little practical knowledge we possess about early childhood development, it's no surprise when you stop to think about it, that there are a whole lot of wounded, broken, messed up people out there.

During the age of psychology, the reality of this phenomenon of damaged humanity began to become overwhelmingly apparent to our dear, well-intended mental health experts.

We are walking wounded, a great many of us are at least. But instead of this truth making the news headlines and capturing the undivided attention and serious concern of the public, this realization quickly became a buzzword, which quickly became marginalized, and soon was little more than a joke.

'Dysfunctional families' was the phrase. It doesn't really seem very funny to me, but then nobody asks me what I think when it comes to setting priorities in this country. Based on the fact that I see things very differently than we're supposed to see them, I assure you, I would have to be next to the last person on earth before I was asked to set any public priorities. I will always put life and people first. I'm just not a willing player in this psychopathic system, and you know that doesn't get you very far in this world. I'm quite proud of myself for that too.

Not to dwell too long on the subject of the development of children's brains, there is one last very important thing I want to mention. That is the discovery of 'empathy neurons'.

In the mid 1990s neuroscientists working in Parma, Italy, discovered two kinds of neurons and their functions in the brain. The first are 'mirror neurons', which were found to fire when one performs an action or sees the same action performed by another. Later it was determined they also 'reflect' sensations and emotions. Observing that same action in another fired these neurons meaning the observer was experiencing a mirroring of the feelings and experience of another. He didn't have to perform the action himself, but felt the accompanying feelings and understood how the performer would experience it simply by observing someone else doing it.

The second kind were 'canonical neurons', and these were found to fire when actions being performed held a purpose, or when observing an action being performed with purpose. This allows the observer to recognize the purpose of another's actions. It is these neurons that are literally *empathy*, and they lay the actual physical brain wiring for empathy and compassion.

So, humans are born with the capacity for empathy. But here's the very interesting twist. From birth to the age of five, fifty percent of our neural connections die. Literally half of the brain dies off. What determines which half dies? It is the half that is not used. The neurons that are not used during that period are the ones that die off, and that includes the ones for empathy. That is how the brain is shaped, and that determines pretty much everything about who we become. To quote George Lakoff, "In short, we are born as empathetic creatures, and we have to be raised as such to remain that way." There's no going back if that window of opportunity is missed.

I think it's safe to say that a great many other things need to be introduced to children during those early years, the widest variety of things possible should be brought to children to be experienced, or those things may never gain a foothold in the adult brain. It means things like curiosity, reading, math and language must be taught, even a second language. To a child at that stage, what's the difference in learning one language or two? This is the time when it's easiest, when the brain is literally set up to do just that and is hungry and ready for it. Children must learn to speak and listen, and they must learn that they are not the center of the universe. They must also be lavished with love and feel appreciated, wanted, and feel their own self worth and sense of personal power. They must be taught to be patient, fair, kind and tolerant, and indeed, the single most important thing that children need to learn is so beautifully easy to teach. It can be comprehended even at that very young age. And that concept is of course the Golden Rule.

People who have that introduction in the first five years of life and people who have not would probably not be too difficult to distinguish as adults.

The psychopaths who bully the world and act like it's theirs to do with as they please are people who do not receive an introduction to the concept of doing unto others as you would be done unto. No wonder they act the way they do. They have no conscience about lying, cheating, stealing, even killing to get what they want. They are outraged at the notion that they should ever be held responsible for the harm they do to others. It literally infuriates them that anyone would dare suggest that they have to take responsibility for a single thing in their lives.

In the bizarre private world of the criminal elite, they are above everyone else, and really, they don't see others as people. They may possibly register some technical recognition that other people are people, but those others don't matter. So it's a moot point anyway.

Once any of us pass through the mental membrane of implanted mind goo and can see the world without the multibillion layers of perception gauze and mind boogers our brains are filled with from the moment we're born, it's a simple thing to turn around and look at those who would call themselves 'elite' and see not anything elite, but something depraved and completely criminal. Criminally insane, in fact. That is the fact of it.

Everything about how these people operate is criminal. They commit crimes on a daily basis and never go to prison. You will never see an obscenely rich person behind bars. They are able to make sure that they will never have to face reality like everyone else; they can install, or at the very least buy off, or otherwise coerce, whoever it takes to ensure that they always get away with their crimes. And they do get away with horrendous crimes the likes of which would put people like you and I away for life a dozen times over.

But there's the irony. You and I can't commit the kinds of serious crimes they can. What we can do is rinky dink in comparison. Our limited way of seeing the world we live in doesn't go much past our own little lives, so our crimes are local and petty, and the violence committed is because of jealousy, hatred, rivalries, small-time stuff. Human stuff. We normal people by and large just aren't made of the right stuff to do all that much damage.

It is the sole realm of the really rich and powerful, the completely protected, to do the big damage and commit the big crimes that hurt millions of people. And they profit from those crimes, because the truth is, crime pays very-very well. But they don't want you to know that, so you get to watch movies where bad guys end up slapping their foreheads saying, "What was I thinking! Crime doesn't pay!" And the narrator says, "Let that be a lesson to you kiddies! Always walk the straight and narrow path, do not lie, or cheat or steal. Do right and be good, because, as you've just seen, crime simply does not pay!"

These are also the same people who bring you "You can't fight city hall!" And "Time is money", one of my personal favorites, and many other timeless social myths delivered in cute little one-liners that anyone can remember and automatically believe to be true.

The criminal elite are very jealous of their monopolized ability to be a massive global crime syndicate, and that's why they make such a fuss over black market designer handbags and the downloading of intellectual property. When Joe and Jane Average do that, it cuts into their criminal business profit share, and if there's one thing they can't stand it's anyone getting a penny of their underworld profits. Or their overworld profits for that matter, because, in fact, they own and control both economies. They sort of have to run around screaming and waving their hands and call teenagers pirates and terrorists, because if there was no one to point at and blame, the public might start catching on to who the real criminals are. It's all such a great big lie.

The criminal elite are revolting creatures in so many ways, it's too daunting to try to count them all. But there's no need to count them. There's no chance of getting away from them or forgetting them, so counting I don't need. Exposing the lie is something I need, though, because the truth of it is, all the veils can be swept aside and people can see, just like Dorothy in the Wizard of Oz saw that man behind the curtain. That's all it takes. A ripping aside of the curtain and voilà! It's just some guy. Some weird guy with all kinds of tricks and head games and lies. Fiction is nowhere near as bizarre as reality, and that's the truth.

It's an often told story how the criminal elites have a supposed obsession with blood lines. Terms like well-born, or high-born, are more common in Europe than America, but you get the idea. It's not only ludicrous on its face to think that any child is born any differently than any other child, it's flatly outrageous and insulting to the majority of people in this world who are not tagged with that erroneous label. But it is necessary for them to continuously assert that there is an actual difference in the quality, and hence the entitlements of 'them' vs. 'us'. They must endlessly propagate all of the lies that keep everyone believing that there really is such a thing as kings and queens who should rule over people because of some inherent right or superiority. It's such total crap it's not even funny.

There is plenty out there to read about the 'elites' inbreeding. They only want royals to marry royals, and so forth, which has been going on for centuries, and their gene pool is getting really shallow. There's only so much to go around with gene mixing in such a tightly limited pool over such a long time, and it's easy to see that a lot of these people are complete twits.

I'm not trying to be funny or intentionally nasty, but admit it. Prince Charles is a vapid big-eared mumbling dork. And look at George W. Bush. These folks are not the cream of the crop when it comes to intelligence. I mean, you tell me what amazing thing some royal or rich spoiled guy has ever done. They don't do much, do they? They couldn't even qualify to hold down a job at Taco Bell. I'm perfectly serious. These people are so disconnected and detached from the real world, living in their own private Idaho surrounded by people born of centuries of inbreeding, I mean, what can we really expect them to be?

It's funny the way it's sold to us that their obsession is with the purity of blood lines, yadda, yadda, yawn. I don't think so. I don't think that's what it is. I think it has more to do with the fact that these people, many of which have families and wealth that go back centuries, all teach their children what it takes to be a serious sociopath. After centuries of two parents from intensely inbred psychopathic parents and grandparents and great-grandparents, etc., where the attitudes of what we call snobbery and imperialism are taught to the children whether the children like it or not, these families end up being completely twisted, hard-wired, genetically wired psychopaths.

There is no compassion there, or any Golden Rule. They do have their own version of the Golden Rule, which is, "He who has the gold makes the rules." It is supreme selfishness and self-absorbed entitlement, it's nuts. It's that simple. It's crazy ca-ca. The reality is that they can't bring outside genes into those sociopathic families, because normal people couldn't survive it. It also runs the risk of exposing the next generation of mama's little psychopaths to real people who are human and compassionate and would attempt to pass those qualities on to those offspring. And nothing ruins a future psychopath as much as getting a damned compassionate streak.

Elites and compassion are not words used in the same sentence. Or in the same room. Or in the same universe, for that matter. They are exact opposites. The so-called 'elites' are anti-human, and if you only observe how they operate for a good long year, you'll be clued in. It's all predictable and consistently despicable. They are criminal scum, an affront to justice, humanity and decency. They revile kindness, the thought of sharing makes them physically ill, and they are shallow, phony bigoted liars who put on the learned act of being genteel and noble to cover the facts of who and what they are, which is monsters. They are the antithesis of what good, decent, moral, humane, sane, rational, fair people are supposed to be. And guess what? They're in control. Any questions about why this world is so f'd up?

They do live in fear of us, and for good reason. We could wake up at any time and see what they've done to us. It's happened many times in history. Elites get what's coming to them. But they just never learn, and they will never give up.

There is a main benefit, the number one perk of being one of the criminal elite. A really amazing perk too. It's a bit hard for us to be able to see it for what it is, because we're just like Dorothy. We think we know who they are and we think there is some kind of magic or power or something special that causes many of us to bow down to these people. That whole bowing down thing, though, is the overt symbol of their main perk. And that perk is that they are the walking, talking embodiments of something called The Double Standard.

The Double Standard is that which allows them to get away with mass murder and the theft of entire economies by willful intent and with full preplanning; but obviously no one else would ever get away with anything even close to that harmful. People like you and I are dragged away and thrown into cages and left to rot for much less than that. The more they are having a field day getting away with not just basic crimes, but crimes against nature and crimes against humanity, and now horrendous crimes against life, our planet's very genome, they are destroying it all, and the more criminally insane they act, the harsher and more oppressive our civilian police become. The more they act like the scum and criminals they are, the more they want to police us down to what we think and say, to track our movements, know our most private details, deprive us of legal power to defend ourselves against them or force them to treat us like equals.

They believe that we are so dangerous to their continued self-serving total control that they pay some of the most intelligent and most devious thinkers in the world to devise ways of keeping us weak and frightened. The natural characteristics and behaviors of normal human beings are made illegal, and so we are grossly overpunished for the slightest things.

This should explain the obsessions they have with mind reading and control technologies, biochips that track our movements, an interconnected national ID card, surveillance cameras and systems, intercepting all of our phone calls, faxes and emails, the list goes on and on. They are so afraid of us waking up and coming up with a plan to thwart them and get our world back, they are militarizing the entire planet and we get to be the criminals. But we aren't the criminals, they are.

You know it, and I know it, and the people next door know it. We all know it. We all know we are drowning in chemical pollution, chemical drugging, chemical foods, chemical cleaning agents and chemical weapons. The list is far too long to be something I could type up in this lifetime. All of the pollution and destruction of wars, all those bombs, the nuclear warheads, the oil being burned, the ships at sea dumping millions of gallons of oil in countless oil spills, dumping radioactive waste…; you know the horror stories, I don't have to tell you. But who is behind it all? Who is it that wants the war and the polluting industries and the radioactive power plants and nuclear bombs, the filth-spewing industries choking the air and the people?

That's not you and I Honeydew. You and I could never come close to doing the damage that's been wrought by the psychopaths who control the world; but that won't stop them from trying to come up with ways to make us feel the guilt and take the blame for it. I assure you, we just could not achieve the destruction these people have brought upon the world.

We've all asked, how do they get away with it? Why won't they stop it? It's senseless. It's mindless. It's suicidal for the whole planet. But it is the profits for the rich that must always come first, and the millions of deaths that requires is all part of the process. To them, it's nothing to cry about. People have to die and suffer so that they can rake in the humungous wads of wealth they seem to need so very badly. It's like the Mafia guy says in the movies before he pops some poor devil that was grabbed off the street and thrown in a trunk: "It's nothing personal. It's just business. No hard feelings."

That's the model, and that's how they see it. Somehow this idea of 'business' superseding human life, and the two cannot be separated, and, by the way, **every**thing is personal, is just another example of one of the most egregious, invalid lies that's ever been sold to the people of Earth.

Every flaming thing that happens to us is personal. What else is there? Life is personal. Business isn't even a reality, it's an activity, a concept. That's what's not real. But they use it as a supposed excuse to detach themselves and their actions from humanity and make human life and all life irrelevant to the task of making themselves richer. As if there is anything legitimate about that. There isn't. Where's the bridge from acting like a decent human being to deciding you don't have to do that? The acts these people conspire to perpetrate on the world are criminal, but with the meaningless use of the label 'business' we've all been conditioned to believe it gives them the right to get away with theft, murder, pillage and every other conceivable crime against man and nature. Just call it business, and you can commit all the crimes you can squeeze into a lifetime.

Our heads are filled with all sorts of convoluted lies, things that don't make sense, that don't withstand scrutiny or questions and that are never allowed to be brought up and challenged, because now they are sacred rights. They are sacred truths, deeply ground into society for dozens of decades.

Today we all believe that we must get up and go to work every day, and that's the only way we can be considered worthy or decent people. But that is a standard imposed on us by people who profit off our labor, not a measure of real human worth or the value of human life. Working for wages has nothing to do with being a successful human being. The whole work ethic is a lie, it serves them, not us. Our entire lives have been subverted with lies and doublethink and false standards that are so stupid if you just stop and look at them, but nobody looks at them. All of this stuff becomes a permanent part of our psyche, just like Cinderella and Prince Charming, and the Good King concept, and most people swallow it without question and never look back. Our lives are stolen from us before we can even develop a person within, and who benefits? The criminal elite. Who loses? Well, we do. Every single day of our lives.

The lies and myths of the criminal elite saturate our world. It's all hogwash and fairy tales, but we can't see it for what it is. We see it as legitimate and real, and it never even occurs to many people that nothing has to be the way it is now. Mankind can make all different choices and have a very different world to live in. There does not need to be war and pollution and injustice and poverty. But this is the world the criminal elites like, because it keeps people hungry and weak and afraid and dependent and trusting of the very people who use them their entire lives and brutally discard them without hesitation when they can no longer turn a profit for the CEOs of the world.

The Double Standard lets them be everything we most despise and everything we strongly rage against for being criminal and wholly unacceptable. But somehow, when they do it, we think it's okay. They think it's okay too. In fact, they think it's their birthright to do anything they want to anyone they want anytime they want. It's your complaining about it that's criminal.

These are not nice people. And they are not concerned with our health or well-being. It is an endless source of irritation to them that we want to feed the poor and care for the sick and elderly and that we want to use our own tax dollars to improve the quality of our own lives and everyone's lives in our country. They see that as outrageous and completely unreasonable. The money belongs to them, and we the workers and the poor just don't need to be okay. Our lives have no inherent value as they see it, only their lives are automatically special. The rest of us are disposable, and we need to just shut up; at least as they see it.

The fight we waged for a five day work week instead of a seven day work week and an eight hour day instead of a twelve hour day; the fight to end child labor, the fight for living wages, for safe working conditions and medical benefits – were long, hard, brutal wars that the rich criminal elites fought hard against, hook, line and sinker, with all viciousness, violence and hatred.

Our progress in finally achieving some of those things has now been erased, they've turned back the clock, and we've been robbed with clever lies of that part of the pay we won and that they owe us. We won those things with our blood and our lives during the last century. It will take an incredibly long, hard fight to ever get them back again, it may not be possible now, with the never before heard of massive wealth and interlocking systems of control of the rich today. Combined with modern technology and the death grip they have on our minds, we're the slave class, baby, and they're just getting warmed up.

They do not think we deserve medical care, and they won't pay for it. That's who these people are. And that's who we are to them. They are true scum. The literal scum of the earth. They are the destroyers of all joy and health and nature. They are so stupid that they don't have the sense to not shit in their own beds. That's pretty damned stupid as I see it. Even so-called 'dumb' animals don't do that.

I had to say all of that so I can say what I want to say today. Which is how all of that ties into the cries of "loony conspiracy theorists", a phrase we hear constantly nowadays. It's a phrase I've never heard so often before in my entire life.

It's perfectly clear for those who have passed through the veil and have gotten themselves some education on the facts of 9/11 that there is nothing to theorize. Our doubts are not theoretical. We're not interested in speculation. Our doubts are here because of a very simple thing. The story we've been told does not match the physical facts. At all. We are not being told the truth. And with all of the lies they've been caught telling, the dirty, immoral, unethical tricks that really define the regime in power right now, the secrecy, the refusal to work with reality, the massive amounts of cash, the dirty dealings, threats and violence, the extreme right-wing ideologues destroying everything they touch with such disdain for the people, such disrespect for life and law, and with so much pride and joy every time they screw someone to death – these people are criminals by any objective measure.

So why are they getting away with it when it's so obvious? Why are they not getting arrested and tried for crimes against humanity, for treason, for spying, for a whole long list of glaring crimes that are just astonishing? Why isn't Congress stopping them? Why are they helping them destroy our country?

It's that perk I mentioned before. The Double Standard. Most people buy into the brainwashing mythology, the rights of kings to rule. The rights of the president and his supposed executive authority. And because most people can't look at our government objectively because of their brainwashing, there is another element that holds it all up. *Our enabling it.*

We don't demand that these people must live by the same rules and standards that we do. We know we'll never see them in jail or tried for their crimes. We know they aren't us and we aren't them. Not because there's any actual reasoning behind this, but only because it is their psychopathy that demands it. They live the Double Standard that allows them to run roughshod over this world and poop all over it killing millions of people. Lying us into wars for oil profits and religious fanatical control of people all over the world who are not bothering anyone.

Why else does this government alone condone Israel's genocide of Palestinians? Why else do we sit still for the outrageous laws that have been passed that prevent us from suing or seeking damages or demanding justice from this government? They are legally scott free no matter what they do. They are supposed to uphold the law, but they break any and every law they like, at will. The Double Standard lets them do that. They can then turn around and create a police state for us to live in, where the slightest sideways look could be interpreted as a threat that gets you detained.

The Double Standard is something we've been conditioned to grant them without ever really thinking about it. It is that Double Standard that allows them to keep perpetrating their crimes all over the world. The willingness of so many clueless members of the public to bow down to them, to serve them, to serve their every whim, to die for them, is the only reason this goes on. Without our cooperation and agreement to let them be everything we think of as criminal and get away with it, **and** tell ourselves they are the good guys, this is the sad reality that continues this whole nightmarish reality.

This is a protective support of that Double Standard for those people and to those who are the most fervent supporters when people like us bring up hard facts that prove in no uncertain terms that these people are criminal scum we are never thanked. On the contrary, we are despised. Literally hated. They scream obscenities at us, "How dare you!" "If you hate this country so much, why don't you leave it!"

The Double Standard allows them to lie. They aren't doing anything wrong when they lie. It's only wrong to lie when we the people do it. Pointing out that Double Standard seems an outrage. Are we stupid? How dare we suggest that their lies and crimes and murderous actions, their greed and duplicity and the cancer that they are on this world, is somehow not wonderful and beautiful, and they are our precious dear leaders who get to do whatever they like, just because they get to?

What's happening there is that we are not allowed to call them on that Double Standard. That's why we're not allowed to call them on any of the horrible problems bringing this world to a point of sickness and collapse that just may kill us all, and not a long time from now either. But we can't have any public discussion of any of those things, or the mind control techniques, or the drugs that are killing us, or the foods that are tainted and grotesque and dangerous, because it's all directly due to them. And the Double Standard means that they can be trying to kill us all and tell us they are protecting us, and it's okay. We are not legally allowed to care more about our own lives than their profits. It's just as simple as that. We are criminals for even thinking along those lines; that's how their sycophantic twit followers feel, and that is most definitely how they feel.

That's why they get so angry when we bring our facts to the table. It's outrageous of us, who do we think we are? These are people who must not be challenged, because they could never defend themselves on an even playing field. If they were held to the same standards as the rest of us, we'd have run out of criminal elites eons ago. It's a symbiotic relationship of authoritarian twits who lick the boots of the guy above them and kick the pants of the guy below them. It's hierarchical, a closed discretionary system of classifying the status, entitlement and value of human beings.

It's actually the legal and accepted way to value human life, and as ignorant and outrageous as it is, it's exactly to the liking of both the criminal elites and the people most sucked into the belief that there's validity to any of this. And all kinds of different interests can jump on board for a lot of reasons to parasitically partner along for the ride for their own purposes. The religious set is all about authoritarianism, and it's so easy to mix the worship of God with worship of a phony pseudo King on earth. Not that there's any logic there, but it's not about logic. It's never about facts. Facts are evil and irrelevant. It's always about this fairy tale of entitlement for the 'special' people who rule our lives however they please.

We who don't see other mortals as higher beings have no desire to play the 'Double Standards for the criminals in control' game. We want to hold them accountable. We want them prosecuted for their crimes. We can see the truth. We know the facts. We know they are criminals a thousand times over.

It's an unfathomable and frustrating thing to be hated for our honesty, integrity and desire to uphold and maintain the values of free, inde-pendent people who believe in working together as equal beings so that all may benefit and prosper. We don't need no stinkin' Kings or people who try to raise themselves above us, precisely because when that happens, we get what we've got now. A global crime syndicate in control, destroying our country and as much of the world as it can get its hands on, with no chance of prosecution or anyone being able to stop them until they're done glutting themselves. Either that or because some random miracle occurs to make them stop; although history and reality dictate that it will probably come to bloodshed and civil war, and even more suffering, death, and criminality.

What a dirty shame it is that those who hold themselves before us as our models of morality and family values are nothing but the scum of the earth; liars who have brought unbearable shame and loss upon this country and who are working to bring on its destruction so that they may prosper and benefit. They are the pinnacle of deceit and deception, and this is war. But they don't want us to recognize that, and their blind followers and fellow psychopaths are all too happy to rake in dollars to sell their souls by selling out their country to assist the criminal elites in obtaining their idiotic desire to have total control and ownership of the entire world and everyone and everything in it.

It is their erroneous, obnoxious, invalid claim to be able to live their lives inside the legally protected bubble of some right to Double Standards for the rich, that is the number one thing that defines them. Because we are all so brainwashed early in life to believe that such a claim and right is valid and even necessary, and because we feel so uncomfortable with suggesting that they are not different than everyone else and they must be held accountable for what they do, just like the rest of us, that they will never have to face responsibility or end their rampage of death, destruction and psychopathic greed. And the brain-washed public, subconsciously or otherwise, will protect their right to keep that Double Standard intact, even if it kills us all. It's a bad case of the Emperor's New Armageddon.

So, a 'crazy conspiracy theorist' is actually just someone who exposes and denies the invalid claims of the criminal elite to have Double Standards. In this world, in this time, and in this place, honesty is insane, because the criminals reign.

Planet of the psychos, eh?

Tuesday, May 20, 2008.

The Cure for Depression

After watching a PBS show last week on the subject of depression in America, I had to stop and think about what they were putting out as the God's Honest Truth. It just didn't ring true for me.

Yes, the numbers are shocking, but they do tell a story. Americans are dropping like flies from depression. People from all walks of life are falling victim to this spreading, debilitating phenomenon. Somewhere in the neighborhood of 40 per cent of the population is, or has been, on psych drugs at some point in their lives. Psych drugs are even prescribed to children as young as two years old with astonishing regularity.

Depression is not the only label attached to this explosion of what we're being told is "mental illness". There are dozens of diagnoses being handed out like penny candy on Halloween night by doctors and psychiatrists all over the country. And along with those diagnoses come pills. A whole lot of pills.

They say that people need not suffer alone with depression, and we are told that 15 million Americans are estimated to be enduring the pain of depression who have not sought help for their problem. "Depression is a disease," they say. "It is highly treatable," they say. "People who suffer from depression should seek help," they say.

They also say that of the 25 or so currently approved drugs being used to throw at the problem of depression it takes time to find the 'right' one for you. There are no guarantees that pills will work, and at minimum it takes several months before there is any way to find out if taking that particular drug will be of any help to you at all. What are people supposed to do in the meantime while they patiently wait to see if any good comes out of dousing their brains and bodies with pharmaceutical chemicals, just shut up and suffer? Not quite. They have to shut up and suffer *and* pay those incredibly high doctor fees and pharmacy bills.

When you stop to realize that so many 'antidepressants' are fluoride-based, it really adds insult to injury. Fluoride is infamous for subduing people's minds, making them docile and submissive, unable to put up any protest or fight against anything coming their way that's causing them harm or trouble. They simply take it and don't complain. They don't have the energy or the interest to make a fuss. That seems very insidious to me.

There is even current research that shows that the very same fluoride they spike our water with causes a decline in intelligence as well, and there is overwhelming evidence that fluoride causes a whole host of other serious diseases and early deaths.

Are all of these so-called antidepressants in fact simply numbing the mind and spirit down until the truth and evidence of the total lack of quality in our lives no longer concerns us quite as much? Are all those pills actually trying to resolve depression? Or are they attempting to alter people's brains in order to resolve folks to accepting their depressing lives?

If the millions upon millions of pills that people have swallowed were anywhere near as great as our Med Marketing Doctors keep telling us, shouldn't we be the most mentally sound and overall healthy people on the planet today? Wouldn't medical professionals from all over the world be knocking our doors down to get the secrets of all the great and abundant good health those pills are supposed to be delivering?

If pills were half of what we're mindwashed into believing by TV sets and our own doctors, then why has our whole health care system's world ranking plummeted to somewhere in the low 40s? We are not number one, get over it. We're not even in the top five or top ten or top twenty. The reality is that our health care is so bad, it's dangerous.

If you really want to be treated for something as serious as cancer and come out a survivor with years of good life left to live, you're much better off seeking treatment in a foreign country. Almost any other country you can think of.

If you're not lucky enough to be able to afford that, then you're stuck with all the pills you can shake a stick at, and all of the associated bad affects, liver and kidney damage, hair loss, sleep disturbances, weight gain, brain and organ damage, and a whole host of barely mentioned but frequent bad effects that can make you feel worse than before you went to get help. And for the last time, there's no such thing as a 'side' effect. It's a direct effect. That's marketing head games for you.

Going the route of standardized medical/chemical treatment for depression and all the other diagnoses is to choose a path with the least evidence of efficacy, controlled by people who don't mind at all that you'll have to suffer for a very long time in spite of whatever hit or miss 'treatment' they start you on. What do they care? They'll get very well paid anyway, and they aren't actually obligated to do anyone any good. The whole system shows an insulting institutionalized indifference to the suffering of the very people they supposedly exist to help.

It is disturbing to listen to the establishment media and medical institutions giving their compelling reasons to encourage people to seek help for their depression. "Every year depression causes a 50 billion dollar loss of productivity in America." "It also causes a concurrent increase in physical illnesses and disease." The entire thing is framed from the perspective of how it impacts the establishment. Lost productivity and increased insurance costs. It's insulting.

The whole concept of depression et al is something that needs to be scrutinized, because we're not getting it right. The establishment experts and medical royalty are telling everyone that depression is a disease, a literal mental "illness". Oh, yeah? How so? How can thoughts and feelings be "diseased"? Do tell. And because of the terrible guilt people feel when life kicks their ass they are offered the encouraging news that it's not their fault. It's simply a malfunction of the brain, and they can throw pills at it to correct it for you. For a very large fee of course, but believe them, they're only doing it because they care so very much.

Do they care? How is it caring to throw pills at it? How is it caring to define depression as a mental malfunction? How is it caring to automatically invalidate people's suffering when they say that their lives are making them hurt? How helpful is it to suggest that, when life is depressing and people get depressed, the problem is with those people and not due to some darn good reason?

To say it's mental illness is an unstated but none the less screaming way of calling it a form of insanity. It suggests the depressed person is not sane. It says, if you're depressed, you're not rational, you're not stable, you aren't capable of making accurate assessments of the world around you or of yourself. Somehow your feelings are 'wrong'. 'Abnormal'. Oh, really? How so? What's abnormal or wrong and who's deciding the definitions of those things? What makes them right and the depressed person 'wrong'?

Indeed, the medical establishment in all it's glory and power is champing at the bit to write you off as a crazy person to be dismissed and not be taken seriously. Your complaints are automatically marginalized and reduced to nonsense. Tell me what's caring about that. The fact of the matter is it's downright insulting.

For all the talk and claims and TV commercials for pills to throw at depression and a whole army of new 'conditions' plaguing Americans, there is still no evidence at all that proves that any of these laboratory concoctions actually do help anyone. The doctors and experts openly admit that, because it's the truth. They also have to admit it since they don't even know if pills help or not, they don't have any idea how or why they might work, if they do at all.

It has been suggested that it's not the pills that help people so much as the way they are treated when interacting with kind, attentive people in the medical offices they go to seeking treatment. Just the human interaction, the kindness and feelings of acceptance and validation can be very powerful medicine. It's well-established that talk therapy is helpful to depressed people, unlike pills, which have no similar proof of being helpful.

There is a great deal wrong with this picture, and a few obvious questions to ask that no one on the expert side seems all that interested in asking. With depression reaching epidemic proportions in America, why is this happening? Are tens of millions of unhappy Americans just crazy? Do they all have malfunctions of the brain? Aren't the numbers just too high to write it off as a form of insanity and an inability to assess their own lives properly?

If ten people all get food poisoning at one restaurant in one evening, that's enough to close the restaurant down isn't it? Nobody would dream of telling those poisoned people that they just aren't capable of enjoying their food properly. Yet, our medical experts and the official-dom of mental health would have us all believe that tens of millions of depressed and traumatized people are simply incapable of enjoying their lives properly.

I'd like to challenge that notion, because it's illogical as well as ridic-ulous. The fact is that life in America for a great many people today is not a happy matter. The long hours we work for the ever shrinking pay we get in return is not a reasonable substitution for life. Being eternal employees who are treated as lesser beings with no power and who will in the end have worked their whole lives and have nothing to show for it is enough to make any mentally sound individual depressed as hell.

Maybe there's very good reason that so many people are coming up empty inside in this society even when they're amongst the lucky ones who achieve some modicum of success. Maybe success in a morbidly capitalistic society isn't all it's chalked up to be. Maybe it's just not enough. Maybe it's not the end all and be all of life. Maybe it's not what matters most in this world. In fact, maybe it's a total assault on the human soul and psyche, and people succumbing to depression all around us is the reasonable and expected outcome of being shoved into a forced paradigm that just doesn't work.

One size does not fit all. One size can only fit the one who's size it happens to fit, everybody else will simply have to make do with some-thing that can never work for them. And while the midrange of people will be able to make due to some extent or another, at the peripheral outside edges will inevitably be people who cannot even try to make due, the fit is impossible from the get go.

When you stop to realize that society is all set up in a preexisting system that we are simply born into, and that our paths and value as human beings are also predefined, and the expectations and demands to fit into that preexisting way of life is so intense that it doesn't even allow for those who cannot flourish in that system, then we're bound to have all kinds of people who are left out. We even call them 'misfits'. They don't fit in.

The sad thing is we don't even extend our intelligent acceptance of reality to those people, we label them with negative judgments and exclude them from the rest of the social body. We don't like any bumps and lumps in our game plans. So it's never the game plan that's responsible for unhappy people, broken people, poor people, sick people, young people, marginalized people who have no place to go and no hope of ever having a place or a way to make a life for themselves, it's their fault. And we, in all of our ignorant, rule-addicted self-superiority, are afraid of them. We reject them and blame them, and we cannot see them as valid or as equally important as ourselves.

We live in a very judgmental, small-minded society. The added pressure of having to compete for our bread only adds to the ugliness. It is inevitable that only a few will really ever win, the same few, a chosen few, and that means that everyone else will have to lose, to some degree or another.

Because we prize so-called 'success' so highly, it's also inevitable that those who are not the winners will have to bear the internal brunt of feelings of failure in varying degrees. Again, the competitive nature of the social structure demands that we never show our negative feelings to others, and above all we can never admit failure in any degree. What can come of that but disconnection from others, even from family and friends who look to us with expectations for success? Our success reflects on our family and friends, and so does our so-called failure to achieve a sufficient amount of financial wealth and the freedom and power it affords.

For most of working class America today it's all we can do to get the bills paid every month and see to the most basic critical life needs that all people have. The fat cats have taken almost all of the pie for themselves and left nothing but a handful of crumbs for all the rest of America to fight for, and there's just not even enough to go around.

What's not depressing about that?

If we all ever wanted to get honest, which we don't, we would have to admit that life in America today is a failure, because the system is a terrible system that is set up to deprive people of any fair chance of ever getting a better life for themselves and their families. We are set up to fail by design. Not realizing that truth, we all get up every morning and get back to the daily grind, and year after year we come home emptier and with less to show for our hard work and faith in the whole structure.

Aren't we in this busy, fast-paced, exhausted society, so fixated and focused straight ahead on that ever-present yet elusive dangling carrot, the paycheck we all endlessly chase after, that we inevitably gallop right past all of the things in life that make it fulfilling and which are the only things that can bring us happiness? When we put job before self and family and loved ones, aren't we in effect bypassing life itself? Aren't those the things that make life worth living and aren't those the very things that matter most?

Over the course of our working lives we will change jobs many times, the jobs themselves become meaningless the moment we leave them. But we can't get another day to hear our baby's first word, or another son or daughter to watch grow up if we ever finally have the time to get involved and participate with them at that truly meaningful level, for years.

And what about the growing numbers of people who are cut off from the playing field and never even have a shot at getting a good enough education to be able to earn enough money to make better lives for themselves? The marginalized people of America are the fastest growing class, and that's definitely not conducive to happiness and satisfaction in life.

How many people are forced into an endless repetitive cycle of demands placed on them from every direction, demands that are a product of our obsession with capitalism and money, where success can only be defined in terms of financial holdings and the status those holdings afford?

When there is so little room 'at the top' and so few who will be able to attain the fraction of positions and spots available that will pay a generous enough salary to afford more personal freedom and choice in life, to afford more time for not working, for long periods of recreation, to allow for extended periods to heal from sickness or injury, that cover families for a sane and humane period of time for maternity leaves, then only a very small percentage of our population can ever have a shot at having enough of what matters most in life. Only a small percentage of Americans will even get the sleep they need. Few will have the quality of life that is required to be able to experience any real satisfaction and happiness in this world.

What's really infuriating is knowing there's no excuse for that. There is no reason that all cannot get their needs met. There is no reason that we all have to play on the same capitalist playing field. There are other things that matter more and other ways that people want and need to live their lives. But other options are not allowed. They would undermine the total control of those who benefit most from this contrived system that brings all the benefit back to themselves.

The sad fact of it is, for so many people, we are stuck in an endless grind of rushing to meet the demands of others, and our jobs are something we have no love for. It is not creative work or work that we can sink our lives into and experience our own growth and satisfaction from. It is work that we can be dismissed from at any time without notice or cause, and that precludes having any feelings of real security in life. That insecurity would undermine anyone's sense of well-being and would only become worse over time.

We work because we have to, we simply have no choice. We take whatever jobs we can get that we are qualified for. We are considered to be, and are treated as, disposable. We work harder than those of higher rank and get less pay and few to no benefits.

We have to leave our children each day, when we'd rather stay with them and raise them ourselves, and that means much more than having to pay a babysitter. It means days, weeks, and years of not building the relationships that sustain us and nurture us throughout life and populate our reality with trusted caring others that we can share our lives with, that we can talk to at meaningful levels and who will be able to understand us and validate us and love us whether we're doing well or not doing so well.

All of the underlying, supporting fabric of family and friends has been relegated to some secondary place, or even a lesser place due to the constant demands of daily life and needs. The chores, the bills, the gas tank, the wasted hours stuck in daily commutes, the going to work even when we're sick, not being there for ourselves, much less each other, it all takes a very real, very measurable toll. We may be surrounded by people, but we will feel lonely and strange, insecure and frustrated, and end up just going through the paces until we are numb.

There is no pill for that. There is no mental illness there either.

The whole idea of winners and losers is a financial framing, and let's face it, who gives a damn about financially based values? What does that have to do with the reality of life, and what's really important to human beings?

We all need to have our needs met, we all need meaningful work to do, we all need to feel loved and accepted, and we have to have justice and live in a sane, fair society where everyone is respected and treated as equals in the eyes of the law and society. We are equals, money doesn't change that. Life must be held sacred regardless of worldly possessions or lack thereof. Wealth and poverty are no measure of human worth, and the very notion of that should offend anyone with a lick of sense. It's a stupid thing to suggest and even more stupid to believe. But believe it we do.

Nowhere in officialdom will we ever hear that there are other ways to do things in this world. We will not hear alternative stories or be given alternative patterns to live by. We will never be told we have a choice. We will only and forever be told that this is it, that it can't be changed, that it's not fair, and that's just the way it goes. We're stuck with it. But it's the greatest system in the world, and just don't notice the human wreckage all around you. It doesn't matter. If you're not successful in this system, you have only yourself to blame, and we help no one by sharing the opportunity or doling out the wealth in a fair way or allowing those who don't fit into the rabid capitalistic structure to have a valid, respected place amongst the rest of us who are making it. And that includes the vast majority who only think they're making it, when they're not making any headway at all.

If you're not rich, it's your fault. If you're not happy in this optionless world, it's your fault. If you don't live up to the value systems and expectations of others that have been thrust on all of us with no chance of all of us being interested in or cut out to live up to them, it's your fault. If you're a loser, it's your fault. However, if you're a winner, it's because you know all the right people, went to the right schools, have the right amount of money and are the correct color. You also have the correct indoctrination to enable you to think like a rabid capitalist, and you have all of the things that get you in the door to success. That amounts to a very small percentage of the population. None the less, if you don't have that stuff, it's your fault.

Well, no, it isn't. It isn't your fault, and it isn't my fault. You and I and all those like us had zero to say or do with the system we're living in. In spite of all the rhetoric of democracy, there is nothing democratic about the systems of wealth, corporatism and power that have a death grip on how things are done. It is they who design the system, and it is they who bought our politicians, and it is they who have changed all of the rules to suit themselves. It is they who are enjoying the system that is designed to benefit them at the expense of everyone else and at the cost of losing all that is most precious and important in our lives. The playing field is not even and the game is rigged. And the distribution of power is nil. It's all distributed upward and not a one of us has anything near the power of someone in our own government, a thing that was set up to serve us. It does not serve us, it controls us and holds us down so that the insatiably greedy rich can feed off us.

That's plenty depressing. There's nothing incredible about millions of people going numb or feeling the pain of dissolution of their beliefs in our government.

Betrayal is one of the most painful feelings we can experience. Being reduced to irrelevance is the greatest damage that we can experience in this world. The wound is mortal to the psyche and the soul. When we see others routinely railroaded in the justice system, a million nonviolent drug users behind bars, children shooting up their schools, and corporate/governmental collusion and crime, and we can't do anything about it, we begin to feel our own imposed irrelevance. It is completely disabling. We go numb. In spite of that numbness the pain is ever present, and it takes a very serious toll.

In the midst of that numbness we withdraw in the hopes that no one will notice that we are not doing all right. We put on a show, keep on the game face and keep going through the motions. But in that state of pain and withdrawal we are also cutting ourselves off from having the depth of interpersonal relationships that is crucial to happiness and well-being in this life.

The quality and value of our relationships with others is everything there is, that's what it all boils down to. The ability to have strong relationships with others means being able to be who we are, fully, without having to fear getting rejected for failing to meet some outwardly imposed definitions of success or personhood.

But in this society there is no redemption. Just one slip, such as a drug arrest, eternally condemns a person in the eyes of officialdom and the rest of society. One late payment, and everyone raises your interest charges. One minor car accident, and you're judged high risk for evermore.

We do not accept or forgive normal shortcomings. We do not believe that time served is payment in full of any supposed debt to society. We never get off anyone's back who has transgressed outside of the very narrow path of politically correct acceptability.

We now strip felons of their right to vote. We're a society who believes that punishment should last forever and one mistake should deprive you of all of your rights.

Punishments are infinitely more damaging than the crimes time and again. If felons are stripped of their right to vote and participate in our process, then who is it that will ever be able to work to fix the horribly broken justice/prison system? Who would know better than these people what's broken in there? We're so addicted to hating those who don't meet our selfish standards that we're cutting off our own noses. How much more stupid can it get?

And what pray tell gives anyone the right to judge another and preclude the possibility that people are not criminals just because they break some law or rule?

We all have the right to make mistakes, and we may well have to fight to retain that right along with all the others they're taking away from us.

Our unwillingness to forgive and help people by simply accepting the reality that sometimes people fall down and can go on to living good, decent lives if not deprived of the chance, is turning our country into a totalitarian nightmare. Instead of our harsh, hypocritical judgments of others, understanding it can happen to anyone makes a lot more sense; and deciding to help people out of the ruts that keep them trapped instead of adding insult to injury with eternal punishments will get us a whole lot closer to reconnecting with the meaning of being human. Our failure to do that is dooming us to a society reserved for those who are rich enough to not have to pay for their mistakes while all the rest of us will pay a thousand times over in advance for crimes we never committed.

There are no pills for any of that. No doctors can fix the feelings and trauma that are the reasonable and inevitable result of living in a society that is patently unfair, dishonest, duplicitous, unjust, judgmental, unforgiving, cruel, depraved, unconcerned with the quality of life for everyone, and who would rather see you dead than have you hanging around unhappy, a living breathing example of just how much the system sucks the life, health and joy out of people..

Depression and many other illnesses aren't signs of weakness or mental malfunction. They're a normal response to unnatural injuries that we cannot get away from, avoid or have much chance of healing from. Depression is what happens when you are forced to look straight at reality and soak it in. It's a sure sign of sanity. Depression is what happens when you finally get real and realize you've been screwed in some form or another.

No wonder the rush to call it mental illness and throw pills at it. No wonder the guise of caring and urgings to seek treatment for your depression to be drugged into submission and the docile acceptance of the unfair distribution of wealth and power that is status quo today.

The only real treatment for depression would be a huge awakening of the people and a redefining of what matters most in life, and then sweeping changes that will topple the power structure and recreate a system that lets everyone have a place in it.

The bottom line is that the only prescription that will cure the depression epidemic in America is one calling for social justice, mutual respect and an end to economic bondage.

Tuesday, May 27, 2008.

Intellectual Violence

Something I've learned over the last few years is that there really is such a thing as evil in this world. True, sheer evil. I've also learned that all evil is perpetrated by force; and that can be physical violence or it can be intellectual violence, i.e., by deceit and deception. Lies. Lies are every bit as much a form of violence as guns, clubs and bombs, because just like physical violence, lies are used to violate someone else's free will and free choice.

The reality is that the violence of lies is infinitely more common than physical violence. There's just no contest there. Lies are the single most prevalent form of violence in our country today, and that intellectual violence is taking a serious toll.

What is violence and why is violence used? It is used as a means to an end. More specifically, it is the quickest way to get what you want from somebody else. You can either just shoot someone and take what you want or you can lie them out of what they have that you want, either way you achieve the goal of getting what you want from somebody else. Lying is the means to perpetrate a robbery or theft. Just like a mugging in a dark alley, individuals and nations alike are violently attacked with the aim of destroying the true owners of something to take what they own for yourself.

The mere threat of using violence against somebody is often enough to get them to hand over the desired things. It works well, because everybody knows what violence is and nobody wants to be violated, which is exactly what violence is. It is violating another person. It's using whatever superior tools or strength or advantages you posses to harm, or threaten to harm, another with the aim of taking something that belongs to them and that you have no right to take. It means overriding the free will and free choice of another person and forcing your own will on them, so that you can have it your way. And that's just wrong.

Depriving others of the God-given right of having free choice over their own lives, bodies and property is the very definition of what we think of as crime. That is the DNA behind all crime, that's the reason that we even have the concept of crime. Forcefully depriving another of their free will is what all crime is. It violates a person in the most serious, egregious ways. It's an insult that goes very deep into the psyche of any victim of violence, physical or intellectual.

Victims of violence do feel violated. They feel the terror of power-lessness over their own lives. They feel the horrible loss of control over their own fate. The overwhelming insult of not having any choice in matters regarding their own life and best interests. They are reduced to irrelevance because of the appetites and will of their attackers.

Being made to feel irrelevant is probably the most damaging experience that any human being can go through. It's the worst feeling in the world to suddenly become nothing, and no one as far as some dominating, violent others are concerned.

To be deprived of the obligatory recognition of your sentience and inherent right to be treated as an equal to other human beings is to feel one's own life being negated as if it had no meaning, importance or significance. There is no greater insult and no greater harm that can be perpetrated on another.

To become nothing more than the extension of another man's will is to become a slave or an object, and we are not slaves or objects. We are equals with the same human rights in this world, and we all deserve to retain our dignity and sovereignty at all times.

No one has a right to take those things from us. When they do take those things, they defy known reality and relegate us to a realm of confused suffering, and permanent damage that cannot be undone or recompensed.

The only way anyone can make you feel that way is by violating you, depriving you of your dignity and personal sovereignty, and this is why the concept of simple respect for others is such an important thing. It's a huge thing. In fact, I'd have to say it's the biggest thing there is.

In a decent world we would all agree to respect the others in our lives and all over the world. We would comprehend the simple fact that those others do not owe us anything. They don't owe us their prosperity or their lives. They don't owe us their property or their rights. They are not in any way obligated to do as we desire so that we may feel happy.

The only people who think the opposite is true are the people in this world who are truly evil. They are the criminals who commit all the worst crimes in this world. Although those crimes can take many forms, the bottom line is that it's always the same crime being committed, the crime of depriving another of their free will and their right to determine their own fate and their own life choices, whether or not anyone else happens to like those choices. It's just not our call to make for anyone else.

That's where we run into problems, because there are a great many people who think of themselves as upright, good people, religious people even, who will not agree that everyone has the same right to self-determination in this world. Right off the bat, that attitude is criminal.

The Liar's Toolbox

Today there is much killing of innocents happening in the name of the good guys vs. the bad guys, but what is never called to account is who defines good and bad. Without exception, it is never a simple case of good guys versus bad guys; it is in fact a case of aggressors calling the others bad, because those others are not doing what is desired by the aggressor. They are the legal owners of lands and resources the aggressor covets, they exist in the way of the aggressors and in blatant contradiction to false claims to ownership of the land and its resources.

The others who have what the aggressors want are always automatically the bad guys, and that's nothing but a big fat lie. It's hypocrisy. And that's always attached to lies. Hypocrisy is one of the main tools in the Liar's Toolbox.

Hypocrisy is when we believe we deserve to have free will, but we refuse to extend the same human right to others. This is a very important tool in the Liar's Toolbox. It is used to try to justify violence against others with all manner of lies and excuses, like religious differences, racial differences; any kind of differences will be used to try to justify perpetrating violence against others when we want what belongs to them. Wherever there is hypocrisy, there is lying going on, and the sad reality will be that a lot of good people will have bought into those lies and will be an opposing force to the truth. They will not be able to see their own hypocrisy. Hypocrisy is a serious, dangerous sin and it's one we should add to the list of things we want to find in ourselves and do away with.

Another item in the Liar's Toolbox is indifference. Sometimes called depraved indifference, the meaning is simple enough to gather. When we are indifferent to the suffering of others, we are committing a crime of violence against them. When big corporations or governments take steps in their own self-interests that result in harm being done to others, directly or indirectly, they know it. That they proceed anyway makes it criminal.

Failing to notice or consider that our actions harm others is not an excuse and it cannot be justified. Saying they just didn't know, or worse, framing and promoting illicit depraved concepts like 'collateral damage' is no excuse either.

There is no such thing as lives that don't matter.

No matter what claims are being made to justify violence in the name of self-interest, there is no justification. When we are led to believe otherwise, that in itself is a crime being perpetrated on all of us. We are being insulted every bit as much as their innocent victims. The message is that others don't matter in the name of their personal goals and desires, and that's invalid on its face.

Others always matter, and life always matters more than any ideology or game plan. More than any government's desire for power and prestige, more than any corporation's greed and psychotic lust for endless expansion. Those things in fact and in reality are worthless up against human life and well-being. Pretending otherwise is always and only a lie.

It's Not Just About Stuff

We're encouraged to believe that crime is all about property and ownership rights and that there can be no crimes without property or life being involved, but that's only seeing the peel and missing the entire banana beneath it.

Every dishonest contract, every con job, every petty theft, every rape or act of child molestation, every bogus war we're led into based on lies is always about depriving people of something that's rightfully and only theirs. That can be property, rights, dignity, life or limb, freedom of choice, or even the information needed to make the best decisions. Again, all of that boils down to overriding the free will of others. These are all forms of violence, ways of violating the human birthright to have free will and freedom of choice in all things pertaining to our own lives, persons and property.

Violence used at any other time than in literal, imminent self-defense from a violent attacker is criminal. It is unnecessary and unjustified. Yet, it is prevalent and it is everywhere, from behind the closed doors of private homes to out in the open in the streets, the kinds of violence of wars and political unrest. Take Africa for example and the carnage going on there. It's all completely unjustified, it's criminal, people are getting hurt and dying, and there is no end in sight. No good comes of this way of getting what you want at the expense of others, without the consent of all involved. There is no need to fund and instigate the social crisis there, which is what is being done by powerful, wealthy corporations and their co-partners in governments. It is being done to consume the rich resources of that land for the benefit of those who already have more than enough so that they can have even more for themselves. Greed is not good. It is just another weapon in the Liar's Toolbox. Greed is always fed with the blood of innocent people, and it is a crime.

Depriving others of what's rightfully theirs is what it always boils down to, and that's why violence beyond literal, imminent self-defense from a violent attacker is always criminal. It can not be tolerated. Not any more. Not in the 21st century. It is long past time for humanity with its consciousness raised and its improved access to education to make the necessary spiritual/emotional/doctrinal adjustments to go along with that increased knowledge and awareness. Meaning, it's time for us to change for the better.

It's time for us now to take responsibility, which is what must be done when we become world-aware and educated.

To posses and use knowledge without responsibility is an unforgivable failure. It's also self-defeating, because it enables that which is not true to dominate us.

Honesty isn't just the best public policy, it's the only public policy, because dishonesty is literally a criminal act. It's an act of violence, because it violates the people's right to exercise their free will. It undermines our ability to make intelligent, meaningful choices for ourselves by giving us false information and forcing false perspectives on us that will lead us to draw conclusions based on that false information. The public will then be infinitely more likely to agree to whatever the liar or liars want. That's every bit as violent as holding a gun to our heads, it's just not recognized as such, and that's no accident. It's so obvious as to be painful, yet how many of us have ever made the connection? They're taking what they want by force and we can't even see it anymore, we expect no less.

We tend to think of violence only in terms of physical things, blood, bullet wounds, physical harm. But being lied to can do equal damage to our minds and souls and can and does cause terrible harm and injury to the collective consciousness of mankind.

We're living in a society, which, at this moment in time, is being controlled and dominated by people who have no respect for others. By people who by the very nature of how they think and act are criminals. There's no wiggle room here, it's quite simple when you stop to remember that the essence of crime is depriving others of their free will and their right to act in their own best interests. Those who dominate our reality right now are master liars, and the damage they are perpetrating has no historical equivalent in this country. The destruction they're wreaking is total, and we're only beginning to see the tip of the iceberg. By the time they're done there won't be much left standing, and a whole lot of people are going to suffer, and a whole lot of people are going to die. You tell me what's not criminal about that. Everything about it is criminal.

These controllers have managed to get a dominant foothold into every major aspect of society. The justice system, the departments of government, the church, public and higher education have all been infiltrated and are in the process of being ideologically raped. They own and control the media and they do this with the specific purpose of being able to withhold the truth about themselves and what they do, what they want and how they're getting what they want, from the public. You can't even buy TV time today if you have a different perspective than the one they want to dominate the public consciousness with. They can't afford the truth going out to the people, because they know the people would never agree to go along with them. Therefore, they either have to shoot us all, which simply isn't possible, or they have to violate our consciousness with an endless stream of lies to make us want to go along with them. And they're experts at this. And we pay them to do it, and they use our money to do it to us.

Every aspect of how they operate is an insult and a violation of the public's right to choose in their own behalf. We can no longer make appropriate choices, because we no longer have access to all of the information, to truth, or to all of the sides to any story. All we will ever hear again as long as the media laws stay the same is only what they want us to hear.

We have only to look around us to gauge the numbers of innocent people dying both here and abroad to get an accurate idea of just how much evil has managed to insinuate itself into our minds and lives. We have only to witness the metamorphosis of ordinary men, who once upheld our laws to protect us, into militarized, soulless, dishonest inhuman robot killers and thugs to recognize that evil is transforming our society from its very roots and defining principles into its exact mirror opposite. We are being turned into everything we claim to hate and would risk our lives to fight against, and we no longer seem capable of recognizing it.

Our laws are quickly being changed from things that protect our God-given right to exercise our free will without encumbrance from power and privilege into things which give all permission to power and privilege to encumber us and prevent us from living in freedom. The lie is that it is being done to secure us, but we are not secure. We could never be kept safe by anyone, and especially not by a government so obsessed with secrecy, so disdainful of being bound by the laws that bind the rest of us, and so unconcerned with our core principles of protecting every individual from violence and interference by the government into their private lives. This government represents everything we once fought to be free of, and then some.

They use every form of violence and force conceivable and have many others being developed, most of which are further insults to freedom and free will. All of them have the intended goal of depriving us of even more freedom, of our right to speak openly about what we see happening, of our hope and expectation that justice will be done and that they will be made to stop. Now that they are making the rules, they will not stop. We are drowning in a sea of lies.

When lies dominate us, then evil dominates our society. We are willingly or unwillingly forced to be complicit in the actions that evil desires to carry out. And it will always desire to perpetrate the greatest possible evils it can get away with. It spells the destruction of centuries of hard work and struggle specifically to stop, control and prevent evil from taking over our government, our country and our private lives. When lies are so common, they become what feels normal and rational to us, we are certainly lost, and it's only a matter of time before we'll have to pay the price of our ignorance and inability to discern something as simple as right from wrong.

We are all victims of intellectual violence, and knowing right from wrong will always be the first thing to go, and the last thing we'll ever recognize. Until it's far too late.

Friday, June 6, 2008.

The Purveyors of Doctrine are Inside Your Head

Everybody loves to believe that their thoughts and feelings, their perspectives and judgments are solely their own. We truly believe that our thoughts and feelings about everything come from inside our own heads, concluded by virtue of our own intelligent analysis, and are certainly not in any way influenced by outside attempts to force those conclusions to come to us by design. We dismiss those who tell us that we are all submerged in a literal sea of influence and manipulation, claiming that we are much too smart to be fooled by such obvious ploys. Yet, the evidence is overwhelming that we are indoctrinated to the point of passive servitude.

We have come to accept the unacceptable as normal, so used to being used and abused, pushed around and disrespected, gouged, lied to, cheated, predated upon and harassed by corporations and government alike, that we simply tense up for the beatings when they come, and then, battered, we go on with our day as usual. We no longer expect a fair shake. This is the new norm.

The insults and rip-offs straddle the whole spectrum of American life. Who among us hasn't been blatantly ripped off by a company? Who hasn't been gouged by a greedy bank? Who hasn't been outraged by the disrespect we're shown when we call for customer service and the companies don't even pretend to be interested in doing the right thing?

The reality is that if you're ready to lay your money down somewhere, there is always a living breathing human being ready to take your money. But after the sale there is no one around and no one who cares. There is no one ready and waiting to assist you with a problem you were handed along with your shoddy imported product. When we call companies or even our own local government offices, it is increasingly rare that our calls will be answered by a living, breathing human being who's job it is to actually help us with something. Getting the run-around is the new norm. We no longer expect satisfaction when we lay our money down. We know better.

The power has been transferred from the people to wealthy special interests, and business has infiltrated government to the extent that they are one and the same. All of the common sense restrictions that kept companies from becoming voracious, rampaging beasts have been erased from the books, and now we are regularly being lied to, cheated, used and abused at the will of big business and big institutions and are unable to defend ourselves. Our government calls it deregulation and free enterprise. It's nothing of the kind. It's a criminal smorgasbord, and we're someone else's free lunch.

We've come to know that our democracy is a sham and that voting is a hollow and pointless exercise. We neither choose the candidates or what they'll do when they're elected, and those who we elect are increasingly disinterested in doing the right thing for us or doing the right thing at all. Our own government treats us as irrelevant, and that is the new norm.

Americans go bankrupt and lose everything due to an illness or injury, because very few of us can afford the staggering costs of medical care. Our medical system is ranked in the 40th percentile globally, a spot so shamefully low that the insult of those high costs is even more outrageous. Greedy insurance companies are deciding our health care instead of our doctors or ourselves, not because it's any of their business, but because they are in the business of not paying out for our legitimate claims, and this arrangement allows them to deny most claims out of hand while our loved ones suffer and often die. Our health care system is broken and every bit as cheaply produced and predatory as the rest of corporate America. We know the government will do nothing about it, because they are profiting by letting this go on. This is the new norm.

The scams and scandals of Wall Street have reached mind-boggling proportions, with so many miscreant bankers and gargantuan financial parasites pulling off patently illegal rip-offs that we literally cannot keep up with them all, and there is no way to stop them or prosecute them. The thieves have stolen so much of our wealth that they can afford to take years playing legal games to keep their cases from ever reaching a courtroom. It would bankrupt the country to attempt to fight these criminals in court, and we cannot afford it. We can't afford justice anymore. This is the new norm.

Sadly, this short list barely skims the surface. There is literally no end to the ways we are being ripped off and forced to take it with the government's absolute blessing to the thieves and thugs eating away our health, happiness, security, and hope. Congress has never had lower approval ratings from the American people who have become thoroughly and totally disgusted with the whole charade.

But how many of us have ever picked up the phone to express our outrage to our elected representatives? How many of us have written letters to let companies know that their unethical tactics are despicable? How many of us have filed complaints with the FTC or gone to small claims court to fight outrageous fees not for the money, but on principle, because the situation is flatly unjust and unethical and they shouldn't get away with it?

Every time we shut up and sit down they win. We are angry, but immobile, somehow resigned to expect nothing to improve. We are caught in a twilight zone of coming to grips with the unfathomable. It's that cognitive dissonance thing. We have no field of reference for a crime spree of this magnitude, for such open disdain for the people and such egregious treatment from those whose salaries we pay.

We're slowly learning first-hand that to trust what this government has become is naive and pointless. We're grossly uninformed about the most pressing, urgent, pertinent things our government does, because the media is the government too, and all they do is lie. Getting ourselves informed is a gargantuan effort, and that's an outrage too. Yet, millions and millions of us who need only to stand up and start shouting still do nothing. Many are still making excuses for government, and many are still of the belief that the next president will fix everything. By and large we are a huge nation of defeated, overwhelmed, distracted, ignorant, disconnected, paralyzed people who have no clue whatsoever what to do.

We know what we'd like to do. What is it inside our heads that makes us think we cannot do what is so sorely needed? How can this be true for so many millions of people? Is it just a strange coincidence?

We all get up at the same time every weekday morning to engage in work to get money. Is that a coincidence? Do we all do this because we thought about it and came up with the idea all by ourselves? Men wear pants, but only women wear dresses, we all know that, but how do we know that and why does it matter? Did we all just think about it and decide it must be so all by ourselves?

We all go to school for fourteen solid years, sitting still in our chairs, facing forward, listening to the teacher, but having no say over what we will listen to. We accept the assertions of those who stand before us as if they were our masters, while we sit at their command, and listen as they tell us that they are the rule makers who know better than we do what is good for us and what is required. We accept our obligation to be obedient and silently consenting of whatever they lay out for us. Even when we hate it, we still go along with it.

In school, we accept the terms of our own powerlessness and legally required obedience to authority without ever considering that no one is our master and that we do not have to comply with anything if we choose not to. But sensible thoughts such as that one have a corresponding indoctrination that tells us that in no uncertain terms our failure to comply and obey is established grounds for punishment. Failure to obey is such a serious transgression that we may even end up in prison.

Required conformity is no small thing, it is taken very seriously by those who want our compliance. We should wonder why that is, and how it fits into the idea of Freedom and Democracy.

Is this really the best way for us? I'm not seeing how doing it their way has benefited us at all over the last half century. Isn't it really the best thing only for those who want us deeply conditioned to accept the authority of others over our lives? Those who do not want us talking to them as equals, else we'd be demanding fair exchanges of pay for our labor and a whole bevy of things that we'd be much better off having than going without. Yet, we believe that to stand up and demand what's fair for us is disobedient or outrageous. It's very bad behavior to demand what's right and fair. It's quickly becoming illegal to refuse to submit to unfair conditions. Having no choice appears to be the new 'Freedom'.

When standing up for our own best interests feels uncomfortable to us, when disagreeing is a criminal act, we are most definitely indoctrinated to the point of servility.

Why do we all believe our authorities to be men of good will and aboveboard character dedicated to serving and protecting us? What do we base this perception on? Why do we accept that men in suits and uniforms are different and more important than we are? What makes us believe there is any validity to such a bizarre idea? Why do we feel that we have no choice but to accept life on their terms and may not freely reject their terms and refuse to cooperate or participate? What's wrong about doing that? Yet, we do think it is wrong, and that just doesn't make sense. Is that an accident?

By and large the vast majority of us accept without question a universe of indoctrinated perceptions, beliefs and values that are externally created and fed to us without us even realizing it. We fail to notice that we are being recreated in the image of good citizens and consumers, obedient to authorities, unquestioning of officials, believing only in the goodness of those we pay to keep the country functioning smoothly. We retain this undying, unjustifiable faith even when the country isn't functioning smoothly at all, even when we're threatened by skyrocketing costs of living, a deteriorating infrastructure, job losses in the millions and two wars under way costing us a trillion dollars already with a third war on the horizon. Will we ourselves, or will our children march off to a war against another country that isn't bothering us and poses us no threat? Will we still be true believers in the goodness and wisdom of leaders who have brought us to the edge of total ruin? Are we brainwashed? Ya think?

We are strongly conditioned to respond on cue to countless symbols and logos, sound bites and pictures, a complex stratagem of multibillion dollar ad campaigns and big media, pop music, movies and election campaigns. Even the sound of a newscaster's voice immediately triggers the appropriate mindset and sets us up to be in the proper receiving mode. These cues don't just evoke a conditioned response, they also evoke a deeper corresponding mass indoctrination.

Voluminous cues dominate our lives, expertly crafted and designed to hook into us at multiple levels and make us believe that we are actual participants in the process of self-rulership. But it is all illusion, because very few of us have created any part of the world we live in. We are not participants, we are forced into acceptance and pushed into agreement, even given 'both' sides of every argument to choose from. Far from being representative of our interests, needs and lives, the provided sides are not there to give us choice, but to prevent us from choosing from all of the other choices that we will not be given. The viewpoints and realities that directly reflect our own best interests are invisibly relegated to irrelevant nonexistence.

Instead of recognizing the ploy, we internalize the belief that if they aren't talking about it, it must not really matter. We think of corporate media as the representatives of officialdom, when the truth is, the only thing that's official is our own take on things.

The entire cacophonous madhouse we live in exists at the desire of others who profoundly profit as they build their version of the world. A world that suits their interests, not ours. A world that benefits themselves, that we have little to no say over, but that we are paying for in total. We have paid for every single thing we see around us, we have paid every penny that makes the rich rich, but how much do we benefit from any of it? Corporate entities have grown wealthy and criminally powerful beyond our ability to comprehend, while we are working harder and longer and getting less and less back from the whole thing. Yet, we think of all this as normal.

The reality is that we are very deeply indoctrinated to be who and how we are, so much so that the mere thought of stretching beyond the boundaries we live within is too scary a thought to ponder.

Is all of this just an absolutely amazing coincidence? A nation of self-thinking people who all come to the exact same conclusions that often can't even be supported by evidence other than the fact that we somehow believe what we believe and so insist it must be right. We conform in so many ways, not of our own accord, but because we're driven to accept and even desire conformity, to see conformity as necessary and good. We are indoctrinated through and through. If we are willing to face that and then decide whether or not we wish to continue being indoctrinated, we will at least have done enough to say that we have been honest with ourselves.

Indoctrination

Endless and pervasive advertising. So-called public relations firms. Public and private education. Television programming. Economics and markets. Political speeches. Religious programming. The corporate news media. Scientific research. Medical practice. Lavish funding and praise for enforcement entities. Pharmaceutical companies. Child protection agencies. Courts of law. Experts and professional journals. The list is virtually endless.

These and many others have established a total grip on our minds in literally every single conceivable way. Each and every one of these things does something much more insidious and destructive than most of us could ever guess. These are all elements of systems of indoctrination, and these interlocking systems of control quite effectively and thoroughly dictate every aspect of our lives, and even down deeper into the control and framing of our thoughts and values.

The goal of indoctrination is intellectual conformity. It seeks to subjugate, limit, or even entirely eliminate the critical and creative thinking aspects of the inductee and to replace them or otherwise restrict them to remaining within the confines and conformity of the doctrine.

Doctrine is not to be expanded upon or in any way altered except by the sole decision of the highest ranking authorities of that doctrine, regardless of the merit, validity or worth of any uniquely conceived ideas from mere, unauthorized lesser members or outsiders. To be indoctrinated is to accept doctrine, not to create it, change it, challenge it, or in any way impinge on its current dominant configuration.

It is always wholly and completely improper to be able to prove any part of doctrine to be incorrect. This is a process that must be undertaken with tremendous skill, and depending on the doctrine, it could take decades before changes are made, even though the need is long overdue and glaringly obvious. In some doctrines, the mere suggestion of invalidity can bring a world of woe to those who would dare express such a thing, no matter how right they are.

Because it literally requires an individual to abandon, alter or subjugate much of the self in order to embrace doctrine instead, it is necessary for the indoctrinators to offer a benefit idea, which will supposedly be of greater value than retaining a sovereign, independent, unindoctrinated self. They will begin by explicitly devaluing the entire concept of the sovereign individual, defining intellectual independence as vulgar ignorance that can only lead to ineptitude and failure in life. Well-honed propaganda is used to sell the idea that conforming to doctrine is the only path to personal salvation, whatever that perceived salvation may be.

Salvation comes to those in medical school only upon the successful absorption of the current and prevailing medical doctrine, which must be accepted as the sum total of all valid knowledge that is worth having. Anything outside of officially approved doctrine must be dismissed as foolish, or harmful, or purposely misleading. Regardless of how compelling, interesting, or valid outside ideas are, if they are not official doctrine, they must be ignored, dismissed and even framed as dangerous, fraudulent or criminal. To even listen to outside ideas is so deplorable that doing so is the same as confessing one's own incompetence. Nonconformity to doctrine is incompetence. Actual incompetence within the accepted boundaries of doctrine is not incompetence, it is something else entirely and it is usually defended with great arrogance and asserted to be perfectly reasonable and acceptable performance. It is the doctrine which must be held sacred, and the indoctrinators which must be deferred to unfailingly, right or wrong, no matter what common sense, ethics, legality, or plain truth may dictate.

Doctrine is about retaining control of the intellectual content of whatever territory it claims the exclusive, official ownership of. It is never about expanding the content, and it is always against bringing in anything new or anything that proves the doctrine deficient or questionable. It is more abhorrent to defy doctrine, or to defy the rules and procedures of established hierarchical doctrine, or to fail to defer in all ways to the hierarchy of the indoctrinators than it is to let innocent people get hurt due to that doctrine. It is more important to protect the myth of the perfection and infallibility of the doctrine than it is to protect life itself. Indeed, the indoctrinated are expected to endure persecution, imprisonment, even death, to defend their doctrine. They have long been obligated to take the fall for their fallen icons in order to spare them the indignity and shame of being revealed to be hypocrites, liars, and all manner of unethical cowardly losers. The strangest thing about it is that people are so willing to do that, to protect and defend what amounts to a sham.

Doctrine is not there to benefit the student, though it will always claim that benefiting the student is its primary, selfless goal. It is there to control both the student and the entire body of knowledge, speculation, investigation, action, and inquiry into that area. It's no surprise that science and big religion are quite similar along these lines. Science is very much a religion, a religion of control. And religion itself, when it is indoctrinated and turned into something specified by others, is also about control.

In no way will indoctrination seek to give something to the student to empower them in their own freedom and assist their personal evolution. It only gives them as much as they require to carry out indoctrinated duties within the allowable parameters and generally disallows or frowns upon bringing one's own unique creative thinking to the task. If everyone was running around creatively thinking and improving on every aspect of doctrine, the doctrine would no longer be controllable, and the need for conformity would no longer exist. Claiming the right to control depends on the belief that only certain individuals are qualified to determine the rights and wrongs of everything related to doctrine, and control is the entire point. It is the last thing indoctrinators of any kind would ever be willing to give up in any degree. Control is essential, therefore conformity is essential. Doctrine and conformity are two sides of the same coin, and one without the other is impossible. Where there is conformity, there is indoctrination.

Indoctrination despises variance from 'the book' and vigorously punishes those who would dare to bring variation to doctrine. It is interesting to notice how important 'the book' is to doctrine. The written words of doctrine take on relevance they would not otherwise have, and those in the indoctrination industry point to their written down doctrine as though it were proof of its validity.

Written down doctrine is held out as much more than just proof, it is proof that can be used to back up claims of superiority. When written down or printed, doctrine becomes a solid object, and a solid object cannot be denied. Words turned into physically existing things do not need to be proven, they exist. There is nothing to prove. In reality, the only solid object is the ink that has dried on the paper it is sitting on. The doctrine itself, the meaning of the words the ink has shaped on the paper, are not related. The doctrine is not the ink, and the ink is not the doctrine, and neither of them in any case have any connection to truth. They are all separate unrelated things, one a solid object and the others are thoughts. Written words may or may not be true, but that must be determined separately. What is not a given is that all written words represent truth or facts. They very often don't.

The written word is no more or less accurate, truthful or important than the spoken word. When the speaker is unknown, the validity of his words can only be proven to be true or untrue by checking them for yourself. One's willingness to believe something is true does not mean it is true. This is simple common sense. So 'the book', whether it is religious, scientific, political, historical, or otherwise doctrinal, cannot be seen to have any more validity, truth or significance than that which the reader personally verifies.

Even when steps are taken to obtain personal verification, it may appear to prove something to be true or not true, but depending on where the person goes to find verification and what those sources are, he may in fact find information that is itself something to verify. If the information he uses to verify 'the book' comes from indoctrinated believers in 'the book', then it won't really verify anything. It will only repeat the doctrine from another source that presents itself as objective, when it is in reality an arm of indoctrination. It can work the other way too, proving something true to be untrue, because the source is not objective, but a strong opponent of the truth. It takes a lot of work to verify anything these days. One unvalidated second opinion is scarcely enough to prove anything true or untrue.

The confusing thing about the indoctrinated is that there are those who sincerely embrace and believe in the doctrine and in all of the surrounding control structures. They don't recognize those structures as controlling or confining and they strongly desire to stay within the approved boundaries of their doctrine. Stepping outside of approved boundaries is something so bad that most indoctrinees would never even think about doing it. To them, boundaries have been defined as something good for them, something that will help them stay in 'the truth', something that will protect them from the confusion of conflicting outside information, which must by definition be wrong. If it was right, it would be a part of the doctrine, and it isn't, so it's bad. Checking that out for yourself makes you bad then, and believers in doctrine will do anything to remain 'good'. They see it all as something that has been put together specifically to be good for them, and their trust for it gives it the validity it will in reality lack. And all doctrine has much in the way of lacking validity.

When we encounter those who sincerely believe doctrine, and we perceive them to be very good people at heart, it is difficult to show disrespect for their beliefs, because we don't want to cause upset just for the sake of doing so. Yet, it is the true believers that allow doctrine to remain dominant in our society. Where we often come face to face with our own common sense, distrust of enforced doctrine lies in the proof of the high level indoctrinators themselves acting in ways that are blatantly contradictory to what they represent as truth. They will be the ones caught in scandals of ethics and cover-ups of wrongdoing.

There is much criminal conspiracy in doctrinal leadership, because the fact of the matter is, doctrine is fully not what it sells itself to be. It is simply nonsensical for any person or group to assert that they know everything about something, or that their opinions are better than other opinions, or that they alone have all of the right answers. No such situation has ever existed. If it did, it would be born out by facts and a perfect unbroken record of always being correct, just, valid and agreed upon by all, and there is no such thing. Therefore it is perfectly reasonable to say that all doctrine is imperfect and must be questioned.

Doctrine is taught and reinforced with much ritual and injected pomp and circumstance to sell its validity, because, frankly, it lacks so much validity that it cannot in whole stand up to any serious scrutiny. There are always many voices who are not allowed entrance into the cathedrals of the believers who would speak compelling and provable truths that are in direct contradiction to that doctrine.

Enforced doctrines could not exist without the concerted effort to silence all those with evidence to the contrary, which can be done in many ways. From censorship to character assassination to threats, lies and even death, suffice it to say that where big doctrine exists, big crimes are holding it up.

The little guy, the individual true believer who is able to transmute some satisfaction in any genuine way from enforced doctrine is a testament to how hard we will work when we really want something, and how capable we are of making due with what we've got, remaining within the very restrictive confines we are given.

What's not surprising is that no present prevailing big doctrine out there today can lay one single claim to any equally big good work done. None of them have created any general improvement in life on earth for people, nor solved problems that have plagued humanity for ages. They will all lay claim to benefits that have been achieved by the hard work and dedicated efforts of individuals, but the organized institutions of doctrine are never the direct force that worked to benefit others. The formal institutions of doctrine are self-interested, selfish, detached things that are focused on the immediate goals of gaining and retaining their power, propagating their mythology, and performing the symbolic rituals that identify them and their claims to the intellectual territory they claim to be the official representatives of. They often do little to nothing for their own indoctrinated followers, not in any official capacity. The direct good that is done is always the result of individuals giving of themselves, while the greater organization takes the credit and the goodwill that comes of advertising those acts of decency, selflessness and generosity. The institutions proper never miss a meal, though many of their followers go hungry every day.

The institutions of big doctrine have grown into a force that has an ever increasing grip on the day to day workings of the world and in the direction we are all headed as a society and as individuals. Yet, there is less justice than ever, and more dishonesty. There is more back door dealing and secrecy than ever, and less open and honest talk that includes and invites everyone. There is more finger-pointing, blame, hypocrisy, incivility, distrust, and division than ever before. The individual is slowly being transformed into a member of a hive collective, being fed messages of indoctrination without even realizing it. Those pervasive messages encourage conformity to some doctrine or another, stated or unstated, overt or hidden, and sell that conformity with less than honorable tactics. Tactics, which have been perfected to a fine art that few are able to recognize or resist.

If the purveyors of big doctrine had anything worth having, they would not need to lie and cheat and engage in overt control over what others have to say about them. They would not demand special rules that excuse their questionable behavior. They would not demand to receive special privileges or insist that they must be treated as superior to others with no obligation to consider the input of others or even to respect the lives of others. They would be far less engaged in self-gratification and idolatry and more engaged in actually doing good for others. They do no good at all for anyone of their own accord. Doing so is so unusual as to be remarkable. What is done is always done for a fee, for a price, or for reasons that are unknown to even their own general membership. The costs of maintaining and supporting the idols of big doctrine rarely, if ever, return that value in kind. The organizations of big doctrine are not designed to give or return anything of value, only to collect as much value from others as they possibly can.

Meanwhile, the individual purveyors of big doctrine are prospering far beyond the average person. Bathed in wealth and luxury, power and control, serving only themselves and those few who control their strings, they present themselves to the public as nothing more than dedicated servants of their fellow man; while nothing could be further from the truth. But then doctrine is not about truth, it's about power and control, and only those who control us can make us believe and accept that truth is irrelevant and reality is what they say it is, not what we can see with our own eyes. To one extent or another, knowingly or unknowingly, we have all been infiltrated by those who seek to have power and control over all of us, over each of us, not to benefit the whole of man or nations, but only to benefit their own selfish ideological lusts.

*   *   *

The purveyors of doctrine are inside your head. They want you passive and silent. They want you to feel defeated and to believe that what they want is inevitable and impossible to stop. So widespread and pervasive are these messages of control that our individual minds and thoughts are overwhelmed and drowned out.

The entire point of the eternal bombardment with 24/7 messaging is just that, to prevent us from thinking and acting based on our own values and reasonable, wiser best interests. And the more indoctrinated we become the less we are even able to remember that there is no such thing as one right way, or organization, or political group, or individual person who can righteously decide all for everyone else. It's an impossible and ludicrous position to assert, yet this is the prevailing assertion of our times. It is only those who are titled, elected, official, incorporated, wealthy and on television who have the answers. It is only they who can create the world we live in, and it is only they who are qualified to decide what our world and our lives must be. We are no longer able to immediately reject such assertions for the nonsense and insult that they are. Indeed, we believe it is all true and that we are powerless, voiceless, and out of order should we stand up and disagree with any of it.

We are in danger of becoming the permanent indentured servants of the titled, elected, official, incorporated, wealthy and televised personalities of the day. The bottom line is there is much more to life than servitude. Servitude is the last choice and the worst possible situation for anyone to be forced into or be willingly indoctrinated into accepting. As adults, it is never for our own good to be obedient to anyone.

Obedience is a fabrication of the indoctrinators who have sold us the lie that obedience equates to being a good person, and in fact the opposite is true. It is up to each individual to decide what being a good person means and to live their lives based on those heartfelt and deeply held personal beliefs. This is how we learn and improve not only ourselves, but our whole world. This is the only way to genuine progress and success.

To have such a concerted effort underway to take that away from every last one of us should be a wake-up call like no other. We are under attack by people who literally want to take us from ourselves and use us to their advantage. They are accomplishing this with wild success only because they are excellent liars and we are conditioned to accepting everything they say and automatically denying everything we think and feel that's different.

One would have to ask what the point is of having a life, of even being born, when we know we are totally unique individuals who will never be here again but are in every way discouraged and prevented from being unique. We are here to bring our unique thoughts, perspectives, ideas, creativity and actions to the world and to affect our own small corner of the world we live in with our unique presence. That is the contribution we can all make in this life. If we fail to do that, then why are we here? Were we born to obey? Were we born to not exist? Were we born to be ideological slaves to those who seek to control everyone and everything in the world? Are we here to not have any say in creating the world we all live in and to not share in the wealth or any of the benefits of our grand concerted efforts?

It is not hard to understand why many of us lack confidence in our own ideas, thoughts and perspectives, and because of that lack of confidence we feel it may be better to just go along with the flow. But that would be wrong. It is always a mistake to go along with something that harms us, cheats us, offends us, belittles us, silences us, disempowers us, takes what's rightfully ours, denies us justice, or treats us as lesser beings. It is always wrong to allow such things to dominate us, because they will soon dominate everyone.

The belief that some are better than others is the truest path to self-deception and the total, irreversible destruction of our beautiful world. That erroneous belief is what is at the very root of all of the pollution, injustice, deceit, lies, corruption, racism and wars that prevent this world from being what it could be.

We will never reach our real potential on this earth as long as we agree to be bound like slaves, mentally or physically, to the will of external controllers. If we believe that we must bow down to ridiculous self-appointed superior others in order to be okay in this life, we cannot reach any potential at all.

That is precisely the reason that only acceptance of doctrine and our obedience to doctrine is all we will ever be taught or shown or have modeled to us. That is the reason we are never encouraged to participate, to think for ourselves, to stand up and walk away from what is unacceptable or degrading or patently unfair. That is the reason for the growing inequity and double standards of the great machine we all live in, and work for, and labor under, and build, maintain and pay for with our money and our lives. It would cause those who desire control of all more than anything in the world to lose their control. Our indoctrination serves them. It only serves them. And it does so to our collective and individual detriment.

Those who control us are ordinary men. They are not endowed with any gifts or wisdom or abilities beyond what the rest of mankind possesses. They do not know more or understand more or see more. They are simply concerned with their own goals and desires for their own gratification. They sell themselves to us as greater beings, but that is always a lie.

No one knows more about the world, about life, about reality, about the mysteries of beyond, or about our own selves than we do. No one has a leg upon us. No one is better qualified to make judgments that affect our lives than we are. And we do not owe anyone our agreement or our obedience. We are not born obligated, we are only told we are. Only we are qualified to decide our lives for ourselves. Only we will bear the brunt of our actions, only we will feel our feelings, cry our tears, feel our joy and suffer the consequences of what we do, even when what we do is based on the orders of someone else. No one else will ever take our consequences for us, and frankly, no one else should ever be giving us orders of any kind. The very idea of others dictating our lives to us is just all false on its face.

We must reconnect with the simplest truths and remember the reality of what life is, and what it means. What's really important and meaningful to us is what's really important and meaningful. That cannot be dictated to us by others, and the very idea of it is asinine. These things are up to us to decide and are no one else's right to attempt to take away from us or manipulate or alter. Doing so is the greatest theft that can be committed, the theft of the independent self, that which we are and are meant to be. I'm just sure we don't owe anybody that.

It's gotten to the point that it's very hard to tell when what you think and feel is really yours or someone else's. The only way to be sure is to close off all of the outside influences for a long enough time period that you are able to find your inner silence and begin filling it again with what you want to have in it. You have to be able to hear yourself think and take the time required to have that incredibly important part of yourself refreshed, alive and in control of your own life and being.

Shut off the outside influences and listen to yourself. Shut off the TV. Shut off the radio. Throw out the big media magazines and newspapers. Stop feeding the beast. Shop local and small. Do it your own way, not theirs. Inform yourself, learn to discern, and decide for yourself what's important and what's not, what's right and what's wrong, and what you will agree with and what you won't. Allow creativity into your life in a very real way by deciding for yourself how you will refuse to comply with anything you do not want to comply with. That's your birthright. At least it is if you are free. Shut them all out, and in a while you'll probably be thinking your own thoughts, thinking clearly again or perhaps for the very first time. It's worth it. What else is there? What else is worth doing?

We will not miss out on anything by shutting them out, because they have nothing that is real. They have nothing whatsoever that speaks to our personal lives directly. What they're going on about is always and only about themselves and what they want the world to be for themselves.

Not shutting them out means shutting ourselves out of our own rightful lives, surrendering our own creativity, values and free will, denying our own sense of right and wrong, laying down for them, and living life on our knees to people who couldn't care less if we live or die. You know it's true. Why should anyone ever have to agree to anything so outrageous?

We can stop the ceaseless racket inside our heads, stop the compulsion to believe them, stop fearing them and fearing what would happen if we stopped letting them control our perceptions, values, actions, thoughts, and life.

We must either decide to reclaim and express our sovereign selves and determine our own lives course or accept that it will be done for us to the benefit of others.

We can live in a world of our own creation. We can do anything we want to do with our lives. There is no natural law that says otherwise; indeed, that's why we are here. We can do anything we like anytime we like in any way we like, that's what the reality of life is. It's in choosing to do what's right, what's fair, what's just and honest and decent that makes the world the very real place we all live in. This is why we have values, why we speak of character and kindness and sacrifice. It's all about making the world a good place for others, not just selfishly bashing our way to wealth and privilege without conscience or concern for the harm we do others. Clearly, the character of those who would control us all is comprised of every bad human quality and devoid of all that is good and necessary, and even of simple common sense. We do not have any obligation to put up with it.

We can do what's already being done in different ways, better ways, or we could choose to not do them at all. We can define for ourselves what is right and wrong, fair and unfair, just and unjust. We can do things the way we want them done. That is our human birthright.

We can do this together, but it starts by doing it alone. By understanding that the world is ours, not the private property of a few corrupt, psychopathic men. We are not the indentured obedient slaves and lessers to those who control every aspect of modern life by controlling what we see, think and hear, by declaring all values to be their values, all rules to be their rules, and all beliefs to be their beliefs. If they can do that, so can we. It is not their private world, it is our public world. We can have it any way we like. That's the reality and the truth they don't want you realizing, and they've taken great pains and continue to take them every single day just to ensure you never do realize it. The playing field really is level any time we decide it is. They want it all for themselves. It's up to you to decide whether or not to give them your rightful share.

Our way is more than likely a better way than theirs, across the board. We the people share interests and values that the controllers ignore and denigrate. We can change that. We can change a lot simply by rejecting all of the indoctrination and instead living our own lives with all of our heart and mind and free will, creating the world we want to live in, without them, without listening to them, without deferring to them, without caring what they want or say, just by doing what we know is right, what we know we want. We can change it all and make it good for everyone.

It's true and you know it, deep inside you know it. None of us can affect the momentum of this great controlling machine by ourselves, but each of us by ourselves can reject control and refuse to participate with what we know is wrong. Arise and stake your claim. Yes, it could be dangerous, but all things considered, do we really have anything better to do?

Friday, July 18, 2008.

The Killing Games

War makes me sick to my soul. What is worth the price of millions of dead people? There's nothing worth having if that's the cost. In trying to understand our society's mindless acceptance of and total support for the mass killing of innocent people in other countries I found something quite shocking and troubling. It is one of many things that directly influence us all when we are too young to understand the greater concept of war.

Toys and games, entertainment, the things that children are obsessed with. Death games, war games, killing games, undeniably frame war as okay, as good, as noble and patriotic. These political concepts are injected into children's minds automatically, silently, without leaving a trace of evidence behind. But the crime is done. War goes on being embraced and glamorized.

My opinion on this has proved to be less than popular. In fact, it brought down on me a storm of hatred, insults, vicious emails and threats from a community of death game players who believe that I am out of my mind and that there is nothing violent about their military killing game. For saying theirs is a game of death and war, for making a small web page to show parents what these death games are teaching their children, this multimillion-member gaming community responded en masse with hatred and malice the likes of which I have never encountered in my life. I have never experienced such malevolence and viciousness directed at me. My crime? Telling the truth. *War is killing. And killing is wrong.*

"Yes, the game is *dark, but...*" "Yes, the game is *violent, but...*" "Yes, the game depicts a *horrible, hellish future, but...*" But what? Does violence and killing incorporated into entertainment become innocent and harmless? I don't think so. Isn't this just another version of "It's not wrong, when the president does it"? Killing is not wrong, when gamers do it. What else is not wrong when 'we' do it? How about computerized rape? Would that be okay too? It's not real rape, it's just fantasy rape. Would that be just a game that has no effect on society or people's heads and value systems, and I'd be stupid for saying it did? The idea of entire formalized game scenarios around rape, gang rape, raping the enemy, that doesn't go down so well, does it? I wonder why.

No, I don't, actually, I know why. It is because you have not yet been desensitized to the idea of rape so that it doesn't bother you or shock you. You still see something sick and wrong with rape. You don't think of rape as legitimate. But, strangely, you see killing as perfectly fine, and even entertaining.

Well, who does that serve, I wonder? It certainly wasn't something you were born with. Where did it come from then? Go ahead and tell me you haven't been skillfully indoctrinated all of your life to accept war and most of this society's standardized forms of 'legitimized' violence, killing and death. Or are you just natural-born fantasy killers? I doubt it.

Luckily for the women of the world, rape isn't quite so easily and handily paired with some noble idea to make it seem acceptable. Unfortunately for the whole world, mass killing is. We have entire, complex games built around killing. Nothing else, just killing. Because that's good wholesome fun. According to you.

Is killing glamorous? Is killing good? Is killing fun? Why do you find it fun, when you play your games of death and war? How do you suppose your subconscious mind parses that out, or do you actually think it can? I say, it can't. It's not possible. Because in order for you to play your killing games, at some level, somewhere, you've decided that killing is okay. Under *some* set of circumstances, your particular set by coincidence, the idea of killing and fighting and shooting and making war is perfectly lovely.

Well, I'm sorry, but I can't come along with you on that. You see, my basic position is that killing is wrong. Killing doesn't fix anything. Killing isn't justice. Killing doesn't even take any brains; any thug with a big club can kill.

Killing and war have been glamorized, justified and legitimized by connecting them to patriotism and *we're number one* – to self-defense and the nobility and bravery of the individuals who go off to war. But those things are not war. War uses those things to get its credibility and its legitimacy, because the truth is that war has no credibility or legitimacy of its own.

Now, don't get me wrong, I'm no shrinking violet. When it comes to defending myself, I'll use a gun in a heartbeat. But I won't find it amusing. I won't do it without feeling it hard afterwards. I will defend myself, but so much of the violence we see and engage in this society has nothing to do with self-defense.

Have you not seen the police beating and shooting people who are no threat to them? The police are 100 per cent legitimized, and so, by default, anything they do is automatically legitimized, even when it's not at all legitimate. Even when it's senseless and punitive and unjustifiable. But try getting around that inculcated, naive belief that police can never be criminals or act inappropriately or be rapists or serial killers. They can be, and some of them are. Cops are just people like everyone else, and there are cops that are real thugs.

That's on the record. Some cops commit crimes. Every day, in fact. Some soldiers commit crimes. All presidents commit crimes. Regardless of any title, badge, uniform, or high office, these are all just people, ordinary people, and not all of them are nice. They are able to hide under the freely given blanket of legitimacy from this unthinking society, and they are able to get away with murder because of that. That's a fact, check it yourself.

Where I guess all this violent gaming loses me is pretty much right from the beginning. You see, I don't consider any form of violence to be entertaining. I don't get why millions upon millions of people in this country *enjoy* a 'good' rape and murder movie. In my mind, that's cracked. There's something wrong with that. There's nothing at all fun or amusing or entertaining about brutality and killing. Violence, brutality, murder, killing, shooting are serious business, there's nothing fun about them. I know, I've seen it and been in it, and there's nothing fun or romantic or swell about it. It's the worst thing in the world.

That's my opinion, for which I'm sure somebody somewhere would be willing to snap my neck. They would feel entitled to snap my neck, because they strongly stand behind their own conception of what kind of violence is good, even noble, or at least excusable, acceptable, all the way to 'harmless' fun. But how did it ever come to be that any kind of brutality slid over into the category of 'fun' at all? Something is out of whack there. That doesn't make any sense.

Some people who love playing these violent games got very angry with me, because I pointed out the violence in them. I'm not putting the violence in them, the violence is *already* in them. This is like it's not wrong for the violence to be there, it's only wrong of me to say so out loud. Well, I'm sorry, *the violence is in there, and I'm saying so out loud.*

Why do they like their killing games so much? Why do they spend so many hours and so many years playing their killing games? What are they feeding? Are games without killing incapable of fulfilling the entertainment urge for some reason? Do war gamers ever ask themselves these questions? Is there really nothing better they could do with their time than have war fantasies? There probably is, but games are easier, and the pleasure hit comes fast and large and is guaranteed. Addicted as they are, they just don't want to see it that way.

After listening to the hostile bombardment in defense of a silly game, it tells me that this is far more serious than the war games addicts are even willing to face. Why should it matter to you at all what I think? Am I a threat to you lot? The fact is that I've felt this way all my life. It hasn't affected a single one of you in the slightest. It made no difference at all in any of your lives. It didn't make a difference until you found out about it, and then all of a sudden it was like the end of the world for you. It's what *you* are telling *yourselves* that is upsetting you. It is not my thoughts or feelings that are causing you any grief whatsoever. It is *your* thoughts and *your* feelings. My thoughts and feelings have no effect or presence in any of your lives. I cannot affect you in any way.

So why, suddenly, are you all up in arms over my beliefs and opinions?

Why are so many of you needing to explain every detail of the game to me? You are seeking justification for why *your* preferred killing game is a good and okay killing game. Apparently, it is not enough that you think so. You require *me* to think so, or you feel threatened.

Killing is not fun. Death is not fun. You're the ones who are saying it is fun, but I'm the one under unending attack from you all. I'm not attacking anyone, I never have. I am pointing at things I see, because they are there.

I am connecting dots that you refuse to consider connecting. Your refusal doesn't mean the dots aren't there to connect, they are there. That's why you're so pissed off with me. Because I am challenging you not to defend your silly games, but to defend your own private lust for violence and killing, and you can't do it.

Where is the fine line that you prefer to think of as a mile wide that separates thinking and fantasizing about killing from being willing to do it? Oh, only under the 'right' circumstances, to be sure, but what makes the circumstances right? A good and noble cause? Whose cause? Yours? Theirs? Mine?

Don't you get that killing is always deemed justified by whoever is doing the killing? Serial killers feel justified … are they? Cops feel justified, are they? The military feel justified, are they? Does anyone bother to think about it anymore?

It takes two sides to have a battle, and obviously, both sides feel justified in their killing. Well, if only one of those sides is in the right, then one must be in the wrong, but which is which?

In the heat of the battle nobody seems to care too much who is actually right or who is actually the 'bad' guy. Both sides consider the other to be the 'bad' guy, for their own reasons. So how do we ultimately decide who is really the bad or good guy, objectively?

When you really start digging down into the nitty-gritty about who is justified and who is not, it's quite surprising to find that so very often whoever is doing the aggressing is in fact not a very nice guy. Often the side that is being howled about and called the worst of the worst people in the world are in fact the real victims. It seems more to depend on who can scream the loudest and kill the most. Whoever is left standing is the victor. But does that make the victor the good guy? Should it? I don't know, you tell me.

See, I ask these questions. And I am willing to admit that it really depends a whole heck of a lot what side you're on in any battle. Both of the sides see themselves as in the right. But if both sides are in the right, then you shouldn't need war to reach a mutually beneficial solution. War is an option that should rarely need to happen, but in this country it happens all the time.

There's something very wrong with the whole damned thing, and even more wrong is how few Americans seem to give a shit at all who or how many are getting killed somewhere else. *Killing others has become the means to feel safe.* Is that twisted enough for you? It sure is for me.

What makes it truly miserable is when good men are called to battle and they can't afford the luxury of doing too much thinking about who is shooting who and why. All they know is the reality that someone over there is pointing a rifle at them in the here and now, and they either have to shoot first, and accurately, or die.

All of the critical thinking, all of the critically important questions, all of the issues of who is right and wrong evaporate in the harsh cold reality of survival. It truly becomes mindless killing in the literal sense. It can be very gripping. Intoxicating. You can totally lose your mind and your soul, if only for an hour, or a day, or a week, or a year.

And this feeling, this exhilaration, the winning, the danger, the glamor of it, if you can call it that, this is the same high, the same buzz that you gamers get high on. Only you do it all safe and snug in your bedrooms and offices at a computer terminal. But you still celebrate your kills, you even keep track of them. You count your trophies.

And all the while you tell yourselves that it's just a game. And you insist that I have to see it that way too, as if it's your right to tell me anything. It isn't your right. Even though it shouldn't matter in the least to you what I think, it seems to be of critical importance to you. Why should it be, if you truly believe there is nothing wrong with killing games?

Couldn't it be that even pretend killing, 'fun' killing, is still thinking the thoughts and feeling the feelings of winning by the use of deadly violence? Oh, yes, you love chalking it up to skill and strategy, but what's all that skill and strategy for? It's for killing. What else? It's not for setting a nice luncheon table. It's for killing. Admit it.

So, please, spare me the "let's debate the game" nonsense. I know the game. This is not about your particular game, it's about *you*. It's you taking extreme pleasure, addictive pleasure from your war games. And it's you telling me, demanding of me, insisting to me that there's no harm in it whatsoever, that it does not and cannot affect greater society in any way, shape or form; and for me to suggest that it gets inside our heads at the deepest level and serves to inculcate people into the acceptance of violence as legitimate, as long as there is a sufficiently evil bad guy in the picture, our violence and our killing is automatically 100 per cent justified. It's warranted. It's necessary. It's even good. And dang it, who can help it if it's fun too? It's just a game after all.

I'd better take a minute to clue in the reader as to what this is all about. Two years ago, I started looking around at all of the online gaming going on in this country, and I'll tell you the truth, I was really blown away by how violent, dark, depressing, depraved and grotesque a lot of it is. There are all kinds of games, of course, ranging from cute little games with goofy little characters to amazing, impressive 3D productions in Flash with lifelike characters and lots of women with immense breasts running around half-nude with humungous swords. As if. I don't know a single woman who'd be the least bit interested in being around sharp instruments in her underwear, but this is 'just fantasy'. No worries about men getting themselves all wound up on bullshit that makes it impossible for them to have real relationships with boring old normal, clad, unarmed females. I say that with some sarcasm, obviously.

Anyway, I'd decided to do a web page on my site about this violence. Not to attack the people who are into it, but to bring to the fore, to conscious awareness, particularly for parents, what it means to think of violence in terms of it being 'fun' or 'harmless'. Because the human mind doesn't work like we love to believe it does. It doesn't separate out what our eyes see into fantasy and reality.

Our brains take it all in as real, as you may have experienced, if you've ever been to a horror film or a really scary movie. Your heart is beating a mile a minute, or maybe you suddenly cry out from the tension and a

of furious, obscenity-laden emails will I be getting? It kind of tuckers me out just thinking about it.

But there is an upside to this, believe it or not, and it tickles me a good bit. Because all of these gamers, at least the ones who first go to my website to read my article for themselves, are being brought directly to my movie site, which is packed to the gills with hundreds of the kinds of movies they don't show us on television. And I am loving that. And according to the numbers, some of them are actually coming back, again and again. As I see it, that is a grand victory wrapped in a prickly coat. I'll take it. Because, honestly, I think I win this time, and in more than one way.

*   *   *

I didn't pick *Warhammer* for any particular reason. I don't care in the least about *Warhammer*. I don't care about the characters or the story. There are dozens of incredibly violent and dark 'games' out there. I picked *Warhammer* by chance, because there are millions and millions of men playing this game along with dozens of even more violent, more disturbing games. That's a whole lot of fantasy killing. For example, *The Space Marines*. Who are the Space Marines?

"The true power of a Space Marine lies in his unwavering faith in the Emperor. He is the divine Master of Mankind, chosen by the Gods and worshipped for one hundred centuries while he sits entombed in the Golden Throne.

The Space Marines consider themselves particularly blessed, because part of the gene-seed that flows through their enhanced veins is from the Emperor's flesh. They are truly the physical manifestation of his will."

What is not explained, is what is so hot about the Emperor that you'd give up your own one-time-only life, shut off your brain and become the extension of his will. The Emperor doesn't seem to do much for you, but you sure are expected to be mutilated, suffer and die to make him happy.

Sucked in by cool graphics and continuously injected with bizarre ideation and glamorization of death, killing and destruction, and the strange assertion that it is perfectly normal to have unquestioning obedience to whoever has the tallest hat, kids will not be given an equal opportunity to learn how to question such obvious mind control techniques. The idea of being a loyal killer on command would not ever occur to a child on his own. This must be injected, repeated, and glamorized, and it is. If that's not mind control, tell me what is.

The Space Marines come equipped with all of the latest sneaky backdoor techniques of conditioning children to accept war and total obedience to authority, complete with telling them to extract pride from doing so and to see themselves as superior beings with the unquestionable right to kill, on command. All in a fun package guaranteed to go mostly unnoticed by distracted, harried parents.

The Space Marines will condition your child to see the genetic mutilation of his or her body as desirable and good, because here it is framed in a way to make it sound like the road to being superhuman. Being superhuman then must be a good and desirable thing.

What's really interesting about this particular toy set is finding a whole lot of occult and New World Order references. You'll also find it chock-full of predictive programming. Children should think of a desolate, corrupted, hopeless future as natural. When the world gets that way, the best thing to do is to serve the Emperor and go kill innocent, frightened, traumatized people on his command. It doesn't matter if you kill innocent people. Ain't no big thing. They're still all the bad guys and thus don't deserve justice, that's just for us. Because we are the good guys. Good guys are people who don't care about anything but following orders. That's all there is to it.

When children think of cities, they should think of them as great places to hide out to kill everyone they can find. Because that's what cities are for. Go block by block until you're sure every last one of them is dead. Because that is fun.

What's fun about this scenario? Who would even think of selling something this sick and inappropriate like a harmless toy? Do we really want kids growing up completely desensitized to scenarios like this? Should they see it as nothing to get upset about? Where are the reasons for asking the pretend soldiers to go in and do this? There is never any question about justification. It's as if just going and doing it is all you need to know.

This is how they get you. This is how they get to your kids without you ever knowing it. They need a steady supply of soldiers, and you have a kid or two to spare. With the conditioning and mind control tactics your children got playing these games, they'll be ready and anxious to go off to war. I guess that's how they keep the good old war machine churning all around the world.

First published in The Dot Connector Magazine
(issue 5, September-October 2009).

S.H.E.D.S.

When you stop and look at the world and see all of the terrible, awful, bloody conflagrations, and wars, and hate, and bigotry, and fear, and greed running rampant, crushing this whole world down into a giant muddy shithole, it's easy to get overwhelmed. Yes, it is very easy to get overwhelmed by the apparent complexity and momentum of it all and want to go get yourself snockered until you can thankfully pass out leaning upright against a brick wall somewhere or in some other way change the channel on your personal reality TV.

But I have always suspected that even the most seemingly complex issues between people, cultures, societies, and even countries, aren't really complex at all. And after seriously running that theory through its paces with my wicked whip of observation and dot connecting skills (the same stuff I learned in kindergarten, by the way), I can report to you in earnest that my theory is correct. All that nasty badass behavior and ugly human stuff going on out there can be boiled down to a few simple truths about who and what people are and how and why they do what they do.

I think it's safe to say that a majority of my fellow humans would agree with me that there is a simple equation in life that leads to much improved quality of living and interpersonal relations, if we could only get everyone to do the math. Simply put that formula is, "Get out there and have a fun and wonderful and meaningful, exciting life, but just don't hurt anybody in the process or prevent anyone else from doing the same for themselves." It's so simple, isn't it? It's beautiful. So logical.

So hard to argue with. It's reasonable, rational, fair. It's honest. Decent. Common sense. What excuse is there for anybody to not behave according to this good old golden rule?

There's just no good excuse at all, at least not from my perspective or anyone's perspective who can see and appreciate the valuable truth in that equation. What's so confounding to so many people is finding out about those people who don't like our little equation and who blow it off like a bit of cigar ash on a dinner jacket any time they like.

What beastly manner of men are these? Who are these offensive, pugnacious destroyers of peace and prosperity on earth to claim that it is good and right to be unfair, ravenously greedy, cold-blooded and hard-hearted; to hoard all of the wealth and all of the choices and all of the meaningful access to thriving, healthy living and creativity and sovereign golly-boy-howdy good times for all? Just what is their problem? Exactly?

This very same question has been asked many times over many decades and centuries and ages, by many and diverse peoples most of whom were probably much smarter than me. And it is eternally fascinating to notice that the answer to that question, whenever and wherever it has been asked, is always and remarkably the same. Sure, the names, dates and places are different, how could they not be? But the meat and the essence of the answer, whether it comes from Caesar, or Hitler, or Nazis, or Zionists, or your employer, your government, your church, or even your spouse, are always the same. Often verbatim the same.

At first glance, and even after taking a closer look, it is more than likely to surmise that the essential problem is a corrupted nature in such human beings; that they are somehow broken, that they need Prozac and an inpatient stay at their local psychiatrists fun house, that they've sold their soul to various demons or devils, that they're Satan's minions; or, for the truly emotionally passively blissful among us, that they are just the other half of the yin and yang symbol; where there is day, there must also be night, and so forth.

I say, nyet. Nope. It's far simpler than that. You only have to take it down another notch in order to expose the root and get a good look at it. When you can get a real good look at it stripped of all the usual fanfare, costumes, bullpucky and propaganda, without the control freaks running around with their hair on fire, without the warmongers for fun and profit schtick, without the billions for billionaire bankers or we're all gonna die routine, minus the 'for God and country' b.s. and other meaningless dreck, you can easily see it for what it is. It's a naked, skinny, hairy little ugly dude, raked and teeming with insecurities, testosterone overload, and truly selfish (i.e., childish and irresponsible) bad manners. What it really all boils down to is this: SHEDS.

That's right, S.H.E.D.S.: **Standard Human Exceptionalism Delusional Syndrome.**

The fact of the matter is that human beings suffer from SHEDS like crazy every single day; and like all mental aberrations, the people inflicted with it can never tell or ever believe they are inflicted. Those who have it worst will staunchly believe and stridently insist that they are absolutely, 100 per cent sane and correct and right and perfect just by the fact of their existence. It is so overwhelmingly obvious to them that they exist in a perpetual state of effortlessly achieved perfect rightness and goodness and correctness about all things and in all ways, that if you don't see it that way, then there is something terribly wrong with *you*.

And further, since they are unquestionably good and right and, for sure, absolutely perfect, pristine, entitled, correct, and righteous in their beliefs, that means, if you should disagree with them in any way, then you are clearly their enemy. And an enemy is a scary and evil being hell-bent on your destruction who must be punished.

And if punishment isn't enough to make that enemy shut up and go away and disembowel himself for you, then that enemy must die. And you must be the one to kill him. Killing that enemy is not only a necessity and a right, it is a duty. A duty to all of your kind whom you must fight for and protect, because they, like you, are absolutely and automatically perfect and right in every way, no matter what they do, and no proof of that is ever necessary. It is never in question. It just is. Period. So there. Neener-neener.

I know you've heard a great many voices of SHEDS before. I know you're hearing them now in today's newspapers, on the radio and on

138

the brain-death inducing techno-weapon called the television set. You recognize the flavor, the argument, the deluded snottiness of the SHEDS position.

Whether it is done in the name of someone's God, someone's country, or someone's irrational greed, paranoia or bigotry, it's got the same ring, the same pungent odor, the same twisted irrational non-facts asserted as solid three-dimensional truths, provable and reproducible in any well-equipped laboratory near you.

Assuming the laboratory technicians are not your biased, lying, hateful enemies who will lie about the results claiming there is no such proof. But of course there is no such proof, which is why, when we approach SHEDS infectees and tell them they are silly preposterous windbags and they are wrong, the reaction is always something to the effect of, "How filthy you are to say such filthy things, when everyone knows the truth of our wonderfulness and perfection, which we alone possess by mere virtue of our existence! You are our vile and hated enemy who is wrong about *everything* and probably should die."

Sound familiar?

Some prominent examples of severely SHEDS-demented individuals include the nauseating and caustic Ann Colter, the nauseating and caustic Rush Limbaugh, the nauseating and caustic George W. Bush, the nauseating, caustic and super creepy Dick Cheney, et al, to name just a few. Institutions severely demented with SHEDS include the US Military, the CIA, the FBI, the DHS, the airport snooping degradation league, local law enforcement, institutions of higher learning, public schools, and toxic waste distributing grossery stores in every city and town in America.

Unlike other plagues on humankind, SHEDS does its harm in reverse. It doesn't kill the inflicted; it kills and makes to suffer the uninflicted. So, much of what we see happening today that makes all of our hair stand up and sends our blood pressure skyrocketing to the moon can be chalked up to SHEDS-inflicted people and groups teeming with the nasty stuff.

So, many things that don't make any sense at all to you and me, because they cause so much harm and injustice to so many people in order to benefit the few, can without exception be chalked up to SHEDS. Examples include:

The US Military shows up in earthquake-devastated Haiti claiming what is needed above all else is 'security'. Why? SHEDS.

Israel bombing the life out of Palestine, carrying on a sixty-year-long genocidal land grab, mass slaughtering thousands of unarmed, starving and trapped innocent people, creating a racist fascist apartheid state and acting like there's not a thing in the world wrong with that. Why? SHEDS.

Oil cartels having the USA bomb the snot out of Iraq, Afghanistan, and Pakistan, with several more Arab countries on their to do list. Why? SHEDS.

The USA carrying out CIA-run coups d'état anywhere and everywhere that existing or forming democracies threaten to force SHEDS back into the hellhole it came from. Why? SHEDS.

The USA's honorable military forces and battalions of high-paid CIA mercenaries trampling the globe, killing, imprisoning, torturing and terrorizing young and old, men and women, helpless, defenseless, poverty-stricken people in the name of a 'war on terror'. Why? SHEDS.

A man comes home late after getting drunk at the local strip club after blowing his whole paycheck on stuffing $50 bills in WandaLoo's pubic hairs, and the wife gets mad, so he beats her up. Why? SHEDS.

The all too common, but totally misguided belief that even though every person can only see anything from his own perspective, the perspectives of others are irrelevant and only our own perspective is more important than anyone else's, and whoever doesn't like it deserves to be squashed out of existence. Why? SHEDS.

Hypocrisy and double standards are what? SHEDS.

The reason you can't sit through ten minutes of television without being interrupted with inane, brain putrefying ads that drive you up the wall and occur in voluminous measure utterly destroying any chance of just getting to sit and watch a program and enjoy your rare leisure time uninterrupted. Why? SHEDS.

Corporations claiming to be persons with all of the rights of human beings when they're neither persons nor even three-dimensional objects, while the persons sitting on their boards are antisocial deviant person-alities who put their money before your life. Why? SHEDS.

Catholic pedophile priests protected by the church. Organized pedophile rings, child kidnapping, drugging and forced prostitution so that disgusting old men can get off. Filming drugged, kidnapped children being violated by putrid scumbags to use the film for very effective blackmail in order to get your senators to give away the country to crooks. Why? SHEDS.

You've got your religious SHEDS, your nationalist SHEDS, your medical SHEDS, your capitalist/fascistic SHEDS, your bone-chilling psychopathic monopolist SHEDS like Monsanto, Goldman Sachs, the Bilderbergers, the Trilateral Commission, the FDA, and many more. There's the military/industrial SHEDS, major pharmaceutical SHEDS, the WHO SHEDS, vaccine pushing SHEDS, your congressional SHEDS, Mafia SHEDS, and the crippling and pervasive mass marketing SHEDS, to name a few in the public sector. All of these entities wreak havoc and destruction on the lives, health and well-being of billions of people due to unmitigated, unchecked, raging SHEDS. And none of them would take your phone call if you wanted to point that out to them.

SHEDS is well ingrained in the private sector too, you just about can't walk down the street without stepping in a pile of it. There's dating SHEDS, marriage SHEDS, rude next door neighbor SHEDS, and gated community SHEDS. There's status SHEDS, employer SHEDS, credit check SHEDS, and bank account SHEDS.

I know that some of you are saying, "Gee, Ang, every word you say is true, but how can it be that SHEDS has become so pervasive? Where is it coming from and can't it be stopped at the source?"

To answer in reverse, no, it cannot be stopped at the source, because we are all born with it. It is pervasive, simply and exactly because it is a part of being an animal like every other animal in the world. Your inner beast is not a mythological thing, we all have them. But unlike the animals in the forests and jungles out there, we human animals have the option to rise above our animal selves. We have the choice to wear clothes and decide what we want to do with our lives. Honey bees, whales and tigers don't have that choice. Who and what they are is predetermined for them. All they have to do when they get up in the morning is go on about their business, which just happens to be encoded in their DNA.

For the wild species, being encoded to be what they are and to do the only thing they can do, which is to exist and function as their species does, there is no time lost and no emotional angst wasted on guilt, conflicting thoughts and feelings or deep seated insecurities. Tigers show up as if to say, I am a tiger, I do tiger things, that's my job and that's who I am. Vultures show up as if to say, I am a death eater. It's gross to you, but it performs a necessary service to all the rest of you, that's my job, and I love my job, it is who I am. Wild species never have to question their reason for being, or come up with excuses for killing a baby deer for dinner. That's their job, and they all do their jobs without questioning why. Wild creatures cannot do wrong. They cannot commit crimes. They do not seek wealth or power. They are not hate-filled or perverse. Wild creatures are incapable of such things.

Humans, on the other hand, are the only species that must struggle to define themselves and must constantly reign themselves in to achieve personal betterment and create harmony in the hope of living successfully with others. Humans can choose to do and be many things, including things that are brilliant and wonderful, creative and beneficial to everyone. Humans can also choose to be and do things that are stupid, violent and destructive, contrary to nature, truth, reason and common sense. Humans need to ask questions about why we are here and how we got here. Human motivations can often be questionable, and human desires can and often do run out of control, causing irreversible harm, damage and death.

The point being, humans are very different from the other animals on this planet, because who and what humans are is not predestined, it is chosen by us. This is the justification for the claim that humans are better than animals. And it is pure SHEDS to make that hypocritical unsubstantiated claim, when it is humans who behave so violently, destructively, and cruelly to animals, as well as to each other.

SHEDS is the product of refusing to control the simple animal within. SHEDS is giving in to the thoughtless instincts that safely go unchecked in other animals. Animals can't really steal or murder, they just do what they are supposed to do. The same behavior in humans, though, can quickly become criminal, because humans are not entitled to take or do whatever they want. Humans are not entitled to exist thoughtlessly and behave as if nobody else matters but themselves. Even animals don't behave in that way, there is no ill will in the hearts of wild beasts. Scarce water holes are shared between diverse wild species in peace. Animals are not genocidal, homicidal or suicidal. These are strictly human aberrations.

In order to excuse their own bad behavior, many SHEDS-infected humans will point to animals and say things like, "It is only natural to be a predator, and predators do a service to the greater good of the whole." This is, of course, bullshit. We do not live in the forest or swing from the trees, nor is our DNA preprogrammed with built-in stops that prevent the mindless aggression, greed and slaughter that so saturates the human species. Our stops are not built in, we must build them in ourselves. Neither is our reason, or decency, or anything else for that matter built in, we must build it in ourselves. Everything about humans that rises above existing in a primal, automatic animal state is something that must be worked for. This requires allowing the invisible being inside the animal body to take control of the self and remain in control throughout the entire course of one's life.

The problem is that it is really hard to do that. The appetites and drives of the inner animal are every bit as strong as the drives of our friends in the jungles and forests and fields and cubby holes of the planet. If we are to be 'better' or more than just an animal, we have to work at it. Constantly. And vigilantly. It requires learning self-control so we do not rape when we see someone our bodies become stimulated by; so we don't kill people and take their stuff just because we want to; so we don't use force in all of its myriad forms, both physical and mental, to control one another. We, the human animal, are possessed of so much potential and intelligence that we, if we are basically fearful and untrusting and selfish with others, can do tremendous harm. If, however, we consciously choose to face what we fear, if we uphold higher ideals like honesty, fairness and common decency, common courtesy and common respect, if we know the difference between our own business and the business of others, our own rights and property and the rights and property of others, we can achieve tremendous harmony and prosperity on this earth and learn to live very well indeed.

But we don't do that. We don't value truth above appetite fulfillment. We don't value intelligence over crony ineptitude. We indulge in our greed instead of doing the right thing, which means, basically, not thinking past our own selves in the here and now. We hate doing that. We prefer to give in to the urgings and appetites of the single-minded beast within and to seek gratification for our animal selves regardless the harm done to others so that we may be satiated. Our claim to being more than wild animals rests solely on proof that we are making the effort to do that. Where that proof is nonexistent, so is our claim disproved.

A truth about being inflicted with raging SHEDS is that those so infected know full well they are misbehaving and are doing harm to others. They know it, but their drive for animal satisfaction is so strong that they lose the ability to care about others. They lose their human decency, they lose compassion for those they are harming. They do not want to empathize, because feelings of empathy would likely cause them to change their behavior in order to avoid the terrible guilt that empathy inspires.

Because losing one's capacity for human decency and simple respect for the lives of others does provoke guilt and calls for the work of looking at oneself and judging oneself honestly, which usually will provoke guilt and other unpleasant insights about oneself, SHEDS infectees want to avoid that at all costs. They become what we call cold-blooded. They decide not to care and are absolutely open and shameless about it insisting, in fact, that they have no obligation to care for anything or anyone but themselves and their own self satisfaction, regardless of the cost to anyone else. And because this is so egregious and unacceptable, (i.e., criminal), SHEDS infectees constantly seek excuses they can use to not only get off the hook for not working to control their baser instincts, but also to find ways to excuse their bad behavior so that they may continue to engage in it without interference or threat of arrest and imprisonment. This is the holy grail of the SHEDS infectee. They strongly desire to remain in their unbridled, uncontrolled animal self and not have to behave themselves.

Having large amounts of money has long been asserted and widely accepted as a reasonable substitution for controlling one's raging SHEDS. In addition to or in lieu of large amounts of money, overpowering physical force has also been asserted, though not as widely accepted, as a reasonable substitution for human decency. The more money and weapons you possess the less you need to control your baser instincts or behave like a decent human being. In addition, with the simple donning of a uniform and/or the wearing of a badge, you need not show any signs of innate humanity at all.

Raging SHEDS is very common in people holding positions of power and control over others, and especially in positions where they can make all the rules. Being able to make the rules is the only way to legitimize SHEDS behaviors and claim they are legitimate even though they clearly are not.

Making the rules can only go so far, though, and much of the worst of SHEDS behavior could never be carried out in plain sight of others, or they would get their asses kicked pronto and be sent out of town tarred and feathered or spend the rest of their lives wearing orange jumpsuits with their ankles shackled together inside their barren little prison cells. This is why SHEDS infectees are often big fat liars and huge secret keepers.

Claims of needing to hide information due to national security are a current and easy to spot example of SHEDS misbehavior. The assertion of a national security need is now made for any and every reason without any conceivable need. It has become a mainstay and standard guise, because it is a very effective way to cover SHEDS criminality or just hide it in plain sight. The tactic of calling SHEDS behavior something that sounds credible and noble and good, when it's really despicable and criminal, has become rampant in our society, and it is destroying our country.

SHEDS is terribly destructive, because it sees no reason to self-impose restraints of any kind. It keeps pushing its bad behavior further and further, and the more it is able to get away with it, the further it pushes.

SHEDS infectees pay billions of dollars to propagandists to market cover fluff to hide their criminality beneath attractive, but utterly fictitious, marketing mind control spin, and sadly, most of us buy it. I believe this happens because people are made to be confused about right and wrong behavior and they are encouraged to unleash their own inner beasts and not make it obey their higher consciousness. We see this happening almost everywhere we look in the public realm. It is hurting us all very badly. We are now told that greed is good, when it is not good, it is inexcusable and harmful. We are told corruption, extortion and undue lethal force are good and necessary to keep us safe, when clearly and obviously those are the very things that take our safety away from us.

SHEDS exists in us all, which is why we all are bound to always try to overcome our baser feelings and desires. It is hard work to say no to an unthinking, unapologetic demand of the inner beast. We often don't say no, we very often give in. If we are not total and hopeless infectees, though, this is absolutely normal. This is the basic struggle of humanity, to conquer the beast within us all and choose instead the invisible self to guide us and evolve ourselves and our species. Perhaps God and the devil are inside us all, the devil being the body and the invisible self being God. The fight goes on. The question truly is which of the two will win.

Those of us who long for truth and possess the ability to care about others will glean over time that giving in to the beast ends up hurting us as well as hurting others. Eventually, in order to avoid that hurt again, we finally stand up and exert the power of our wiser self and tell our inner beast, "No."

Sometimes that means having a minute to minute struggle of higher mind against ravenous beast that is protracted and exhausting. Often it only means holding firm until the struggle diminishes. Either way it's never fun. But to never attempt to control the beast at all, for any number of excuses or selfish reasons, turns the better self into a beast of its own, and the two teamed together in beastly form can do nothing but wreak havoc on our world, causing senseless harm to innocent others, mindlessly defiling and destroying the beauty, dignity and possibilities that being human can afford. It's a choice we all have to make, over and over again.

The inner beast never stops nagging us, confusing us, tugging at us, filling us with guiltless desire; but if consistently told 'no', it will over time shut up. It can never go away, it is literally a part of our physical being, but it can be trained, like many other animals can be trained, to obey our commands, to serve the will of our better selves, and in doing so it can cease to be merely a physical shell for the human animal. It can become a fitting physical embodiment for the higher self, the spiritual self, the human being. At least that's something to shoot for.

We don't need to judge each other too awfully harshly for not being perfect accomplished totally evolved beings. We all need help learning how to handle existing in this crazy world. Some of us are lucky to have all the help in the world, while many of us have little in the way of help. Many of us grow up undermined, sabotaged outright, living in environments where thinking is extremely indoctrinated and calcified and where different ideas are not welcomed. Many of us must exist in environments where everyone is conditioned to behave in certain ways and we are expected and required to go along with that conditioning even when we can see that it's wrong or harmful or unjust. It's a conundrum for those among us who know there is more, that we are all capable of more, and that engaging the mind and soul is only a heartbeat away and that doing so would bring so much light to the world, it's not even funny.

We have to be patient, tolerant and aware, but not stupid, and we have to try to teach each other and cut each other reasonable slack. We also have to try not to be so full of ourselves that we forget that we too struggle with our own beast every single day of our lives. Nobody is perfect, and anyone who claims to be perfect should be held at arm's length and ridiculed loudly for their silliness.

The people who we shouldn't be quite so patient with in their struggles with SHEDS are those who affect the lives of countless others. No right can exist or ever shall exist to cause harm or unwanted change to others' lives and well-being against their will or without their knowledge and consent, and yet, it seems our 'government' does little else these days. No one should ever be elevated to positions where they may harm others at will without full accountability or for personal gain. No one should ever be allowed to perpetrate crimes without fear of prosecution. The increasing existence of these things is the vulgar proof that SHEDS has infected our society and if not stopped, it will utterly consume us. To allow that to happen is nothing more than stupid. We are not stupid. But SHEDS-infected persons become stupid, and when a SHEDS pandemic is underway, it causes mass stupidity to rule our lives.

The list of private individuals and businesses and public, governmental and nonprofit institutions utterly saturated with SHEDS is far too numerous to list. They cannot all be listed, but it's not important to make up a master list. What is important is learning to recognize SHEDS in order to call it for what it is. What is important is to explain SHEDS to your friends, family and loved ones, to your coworkers, cab drivers and school teachers, to your friendlier cops, lawyers and judges, so that they too will begin to see the SHEDS everywhere they look and they too will be able to stand up, point and call out, "SHEDS!" Just like a white-tailed deer signals its fellow white-tailed deer so all may bolt in every direction all at once in order to avoid the stalking predator in their midst and save their lives. Learning to recognize SHEDS, then pointing right at it and calling out, "SHEDS!", would without a doubt in the mind of this writer do untold good for all humankind. Our simple refusal to be duped by the lies of SHEDS-infected others would systematically, nonviolently, and invariably bring an end to the terrible, raging SHEDS pandemic enveloping the globe today.

Thursday, January 28, 2010.

Broken Wheel

I won't deny it, sometimes I can get dang depressed about the endless stream of evil things happening in our bruised and broken little world, much of the worst of which comes at the hands of our own dear incorporated govmint. I can also get sorely depressed about my own personal life; I could give you a whole long list of things that have gone wrong, mistakes I've made, things that should never have happened, but did happen, encounters with predators and thugs of all kinds, getting ripped off, used and disrespected... You know, life. I have taken my share of damage, maybe more than some, maybe less than others, but damage happened.

It can be painful to understand accumulated damage in retrospect, knowing there is nothing I can do about it now. I can't go back in time and relive something and make sure it comes out right this time, or make sure it doesn't happen this time, or be braver this time or less gullible, whatever it is that I think would have kept me from taking on another brick in my private wall of hurt. A private wall, which, my guess is, everybody has.

If you're living, you're going to get hurt; in fact, if you're not getting hurt, you're not doing much living. Private walls encircle us all, built from the bricks of life experience. Maybe we use these walls to protect ourselves, but it's just as likely they could imprison us instead. A real danger lies in becoming so imprisoned behind our private walls of pain that we can no longer see anything beyond them; all we can see are those awful bricks, each one imprinted with the indelible story that placed it there. It does hurt to lose irreplaceable things like time and health and trust and hope, fill in the blanks with your own words. It can be hard to sit in peace with the knowledge that life shouldn't have been this way and it wouldn't have been this way, if only…

If only what? If only we'd had different parents, a different family, a different education? If only we'd been born in a different place or in a different time? If only we'd had enough money to overcome some of the uglier roadblocks to happiness, maybe then we wouldn't feel like we got into a fight with life and lost. But would any of those possibilities really have prevented us from getting hurt in this life? Honestly? I very much doubt it.

Being undermined, used, cheated, lied to, violated… Again, fill in the blanks as you please, these kinds of things shouldn't be the structural underlying factors of anyone's life, but I'm sorry to say, I think they often are. It would seem they'd provide precious little to build a life on. Wouldn't you think that only by extricating oneself from these types of things could one begin to clear a space for a personal foundation on which to build an actual life? And wouldn't never having these things crop up in the first place be even better?

It would be like the difference between being handed a broken wheel at the start of a race or one that isn't broken. A broken wheel is useless. You don't know how to repair it. You don't have the knowledge or the skills to know how to fix it, but unless you can make it work, you won't be going anywhere, so you have to try to do what you can. You try this and that, it doesn't work, time whizzes by, finite resources are strained to depletion. You take bad advice from good people and bad advice from bad people and end up with things worse than they already were. You are painfully aware that you must fully invest every bit of yourself just to get that broken wheel into a basic, usable state, while in the meantime you're not covering any ground, you're just continually struggling with a frustrating situation that is only made worse when you can see the guy next to you getting handed a beautiful brand new wheel that is not broken; and he sets it down and hollers, "Weeee!" – and off he goes. It's doubly insulting when you know the guy is a moron and a genuine jerk.

For that guy, deserving or otherwise, life is good. He probably can't conceive of what it's like to be handed a broken wheel that doesn't work and won't go anywhere, and you can't fix it, and it all sucks and never stops sucking. He has no frame of reference for that sort of thing, it isn't in his life experience. He may not be a bad person at all, just a person who has zero understanding of something he's never been through himself. Which only makes sense.

But then again, maybe he knows full well that he just got handed the sweet and easy ticket to success. For him other people's troubles and their broken wheels are their own problem. He's probably even glad that your wheel is broken. Hell, plenty of people out there spend all day long trying to figure out how to break other people's wheels. They understand it's an unbeatable handicap to run in a race against people who have no feet. Some would even hire others to cut the competition's feet off, and there are always those happy to show up and take the money and do it. Think Nancy Kerrigan for a literal example of that metaphor.

Dishonorable people are a dime a dozen in this world. It grinds my craw (whatever a craw is) whenever I see people like that win, and the fact of it is people like that win all the time. Crime does pay. It pays extremely well. In fact, it's the only thing that does pay extremely well. You and I were told just the opposite, we were told that crime never pays. That was just one of the million lies they tell us during our for- mative years, and that one's right up there with "Wonderbread builds strong bodies in twelve ways". The criminals of culture are experts at breaking other people's wheels, if nothing else. They excel at pulling off dirty deeds, and they're never bothered by conscience over it. On the contrary, they're very pleased with themselves. The real geniuses at it can turn abject filth into some noble sounding thing, and people will not see the filth and will instead give them a standing ovation and a prize. I'm telling ya, it is scary out there in the real world. Things are next to never what they seem, and they are definitely never what we're told they are.

It doesn't seem right that bad people win so often. Where is the justice in this universe, when nasty, mean and selfish people take all and good people have to suck mud and die? That might well be the question that spawned conformist religiosity so long ago; and who else would step in to play the lead role and answer that question but the very same people who made folks ask it in the first place?

I put it to you that this obnoxious, offensive paradigm is status quo with our species. I'm saying this is nothing new, in fact, it's as old as the hills. It has always been like this, no matter when you were born or where. It would be very rare and unusual, if not impossible, to not have to run the whole gauntlet of oppressive negative forces restricting most people's lives, confining every life to be lived inside boundaries that are invariably asserted as real and legitimate when they're neither, defined as normal when they're not, and set and enforced by external, unknown others without you getting any say in the matter at all.

Society at large simply accepts this status quo, and not passively. They deeply accept it at face value and believe only what they are told to believe about it. They will attack anyone who actually thinks about it, analyzes it, or questions it. They will also happily kill anyone who refuses to be enslaved by the lies and manipulations that turn entire nations into intellectually and emotionally disconnected children living inside grown up bodies.

What a setup. It's an eternally repeating loop. It's the perfect recipe to protect those who feed on others, those who lie, cheat, steal and manipulate while simultaneously ensuring a steady supply of willing victims.

The parasite clown kings of earth hoist themselves and each other onto all the highest of the high public pedestals for every last sheeple to look upon and worship. All it takes is walling in the minds of people from childhood, never showing them anything beyond the props that are used in the daily production and denying there is anything beyond those props, should anything else be inadvertently dragged in. The mind is thus imprisoned, and when it is imprisoned, it ceases to be, because when it thinks it knows all there is to know, it stops thinking. It stops asking questions. It stops seeking. It stops learning. It stops caring. And it resists worthwhile change. Change would mean the answers you already possess are wrong. A shut off mind can't adapt. It cannot change.

That might be why bringing new information to the old table is often a total waste of time and can be about as welcome as the plague. All the hard facts in the world won't penetrate the brain of someone who has stopped thinking.

Are you with me so far? You are? Great! Then roll down your socks into ankle donuts and follow me back to the broken wheel scenario.

It is flat understandable that being handed a broken wheel in life can cause some serious unhappiness. Especially when we can see the blatantly unfair way that certain other people are predictably and invariably handed beautiful brand new unbroken wheels.

But here's the thing. Did you ask for a wheel? Did you desire to be entered into someone else's race? Are their rules of any interest to you? Do they mean anything in your life? Why would you want someone else to hand you a wheel in the first place? Especially when it's clear that what they're handing you is a rigged game, a handicap, something that will hold you back while helping someone else win this rigged race? It's a perfectly good question to ask: what's in it for me? Whose game are we playing here and why?

It is true that for the most part we don't have much choice about being in 'the race'. If you want to eat, if you want to fit in, if you don't want to be called a loser and a freak and be rejected from inclusion in the action and activity around you that does everything from get you food and shelter to friends to sex to love to choices of ways to spend your time and life, then you are essentially forced to get in the race and pedal where they tell you to go. But you don't have to buy into it, and you don't have to believe in it, and most of all you don't have to accept it as it is and just go along. You don't have to take anyone's broken wheel onto yourself. You can say, "No, thanks, I'm making and using my own wheel, it's one of a kind and it's mine all mine." If you're a thinking person, you have to get to the point where you realize what nonsense everything in the phony rat race is and how truly little the blabbering, posturing, plastic circus of fools have to offer that has any real value, substance, or meaning. And I think, when you realize that, that is the moment, or at least the beginning of the metamorphosis, that honest to goodness sets you free.

You can't get to here without going there first. Broken wheels open your eyes. Then you can finally see. What matters is not what they're doing out there, but what you think matters. That is an immovable truth that 'they' cannot do anything about. They know this, it is not a news flash by any stretch. They know it exquisitely well. They know that all it would take to blow their whole False World of the Parasite Clowns to pieces is enough people thinking like this.

With enough people seeing right through them not a shot would need to be fired. No riots would occur. In an atmosphere of peaceful silence their games and all of their lies and senseless ways would become like melting snow. They would no longer control the race. They would no longer control the outcome. They would no longer control anything.

But that will never happen. At least not in my lifetime. I don't see much chance of millions of people who can no longer think on their own getting to the point where they can see truth they've been told does not exist. They are literally hypnotized and can only see what they're told is there to see. Love those people, be kind to them, but don't waste time trying to jump-start their minds, and don't turn your back to them, because they just might drive a knife through it. Why? Because instead of thinking and perceiving the world around them, they live in perpetual fear. And nothing gets fearful people more excited than something coming along that sounds like change. Different is bad, it doesn't matter a whit if it's true.

If you think about it, it only makes perfect sense. If you don't know anything about the world you live in beyond what you've been told by others, you will live in fear. People fear the unknown, and the real world that exists beyond their own lives is literally unknown to them. They would deny that, of course, but that won't change the fact. Ignorance, or denial, or even straight-out dishonesty, cannot change what is true. What is true will be true whether we know it or not, or like it or not, or agree with it or not. It will be true even if we say something else is true instead. Nothing we do will touch what is true. What is true cannot be changed by anything we say or do.

This is probably why so much time, energy and money is spent on covering up, literally burying what is true and then asserting that something else is true instead. It is most often done by laying something else on top of the truth to partially or completely obscure it. When people ask, "What is true", they will point and say, "Here is where the truth is, come and see it for yourself. We will show it to you." And they will point to where the truth is said to reside, and people will look and what they will see is what has been laid on top of the truth. Then they will say, "Now we know what is true." Only they won't know what is true, and they'll probably never figure that out. It's not exactly impressive or complicated to throw a whole lot of people off the trail of truth. It is devious and dishonest, though. And it's par for the course. Anywhere there is money flowing, there is a sea of bullshit to float it on. Show me one exception, and I'll eat my hat.

But you know what? I think that deep down inside people know they don't have the real truth. They just can't stand the idea of it. A shut-down mind doesn't want anything to change.

People usually don't like change anyway, at least not when the status quo is comfy enough to tolerate and the rewards for playing the game keep coming in. A state of ignorance is a matter of will, not a matter of truth. Deep inside, where truth rings like a bell, they don't hear that ringing. They hear lots of circus music and talking heads and assertions played on endless repeating loops and they're told that unless everything stays the way it is then everything would fall apart and chaos and anarchy would turn the planet into literal hell. People see the finger-pointing and stage-show posturing, but they don't hear that ring of truth.

The closer they get to noticing that and asking themselves what it means, then the closer they get to the most important fork in the road of a lifetime. Do they strike out on their own and begin searching for the truth, or do they choose to remain ignorant by dismissing all available information and demanding they are right and everyone else is wrong?

If they decide to remain ignorant, it is because it pays to remain ignorant. It's much easier, it is effortless, in fact, and since you're making everything up as you go, then you can also make up the idea that you're right.

If they decide to strike out on their own and hunt for the truth, we'll probably never hear from them again, because they'll be dang busy for the rest of their lives. Regardless of the choices made, the truth will never go away. Ever. It will always be there, it is always there to be discovered and understood. Ignoring it won't change it. Denying it won't change it. Hiding it won't change it. It will always be there.

Thursday, November 18, 2010.

Spare Me

Oh, please. Spare me your drama queen finger-pointing judgment of my being. What do you know of me? Not a thing. You stand there with that look on your face, calling me racist, or antisemitic, or unpatriotic, or any other knee-jerking self-superior subjective judgment of my person, and all of your nose in the air bluster is nothing but hot air. It is playacting. It is caustic, insulting, divisive, unhelpful, illogical, unwarranted, and plain stupid. What is the matter with you?

You're not fooling me or scaring me or making me recoil in horror for fear of your branding me with your mark of some sort of politically correct Zorro, carving a big R for racist with a circle around it on my forehead for all to see. Your cartoon tattoos of judgment are a plastic joke. The only thing about you that is real is your viciousness towards others. And you're supposed to be so much better than the rest of us? You can't even respect people with a different opinion than yours. What's so superior about that? That is the bottom of the barrel in human attitudes, my friend. It's called intolerance, it's bigotry. You are what you rail so loudly against. I don't care how self-superior you feel, you are not the end all and be all of human perfection. Who told you that you were? What are your qualifications for this lofty self-image? You don't have any qualifications, and according to you, you apparently don't need any. Your personal sense of superiority comes from nothing more than a bloated, overbearing intolerance for all who are not just like you. Well, my goodness, you're just as imperfect as the very people you are so quick to judge.

People, I ask you, where's Gandhi when you need him? Where is any natural man with a lick of sense who knows the difference between a bag of hot air and a hole in the ground? Where are the shepherds of the soul with the visionary messages that raise the human consciousness as opposed to shoving its face down into the dreck and the mud of ignorance and fear and selfishness? Where are the voices of men who lift us to something higher by speaking to us of humility and appreciation and mutual respect? Where are all of those voices? Are they all dead? All of them? How did that happen?

Where is the common sense? 'Common sense' is an oxymoron, it's not common at all. It's quite uncommon. It is so uncommon, in fact, that the universe has to send us occasional exemplars of common sense, light bringers, those with the gift of genuine superiority that is always and only revealed by true humility and undying courage, by selfless generosity, kindness, patience, fairness and honesty, and never by self-appointed, self-aggrandizing trumpet blaring, wealth-accumulating, gun-toting general announcement.

It is hard not to notice that the most hated people on earth have often been those who simply tell the truth. You can get killed for that you know. It seems that truth is something that most people don't want to hear. People prefer to be lied to. They want to be told stories that support the pink bubble they live in, stories about how superior they are, or what victims they are, or how brilliant, entitled, deserving, educated and sophisticated they are. People want to hear that they're special, that they're better than other people, even that their version of God told them so, so it must be true.

As a brief aside, if your version of God says that 'your people' (whatever that means) are superior to all other people on earth, what was the point? Why would the almighty being, the creator of all that is, an intelligence so profound and so beyond you that you cannot even fathom it, what point would there be in this being's mind to singling out one stripe of humanity and telling them he favors them?

If God the Almighty didn't like the rest of his human creation, he wouldn't need your help to get rid of them. He could handle that himself. If he created them, he could uncreate them, but that hasn't happened, and it never will. So maybe it's not that God singled you out to dote on, spoil and favor so much as he singled you out to hold responsible. Maybe he expects better from you, because he knows you can do better. And maybe, just maybe, your interpretation of being 'chosen' does not equate to you being given permission to act like the most violent scum of the earth in existence and get away with it. Maybe it really means you're supposed to do God's work for him, which, as previously noted, is not to exterminate everyone but yourself.

But you can't handle that, can you. You? Keeping all of God's Ten Commandments? That will be the day. *Thou shalt not kill* is just too much to give up. You like killing. Face it, you like killing. You know it's wrong, but you just tell yourself that you're killing for God/country and you feel superior and entitled to go kill people. Here's a tip for you, you missed the mark on this one. Your God, should he really exist, will definitely be filling you in when you get to your version of heaven.

There must be a special place in hell for those deluded souls who break every law of God and man in the belief it is God's will for them to do so. Is insanity punishable by eternity in the fires of hell? Only if it's insanity by choice. Insanity by lazy following of the rabid herd. Insanity by refusal to use the brains and the heart God gave you. Short answer, yep, you're going to hell. And all of you anal probing torturing scum bags for God & country, I hope you like pitchforks, because you'll have one up your ass for the rest of all time. Now that's patriotic. And Godly too.

To pick up where I left off before, I was saying how it's hard not to notice that when people are demonized and vilified in the press, when it reaches a point of total saturation and orgasmic hate and fear, chances are near 100 per cent certainty that the object(s) of all that hate and fear are neither demonic nor villainous. They are not inhuman or ungodly people. They are not like animals. They do not hate us for our beliefs and ways. They are not out to get us. They do not eat our flesh or drink human blood. They do not take babies out of incubators and leave them on cold floors to die. They are not rabid haters of little old innocent us, nor have most of them even heard of us. Indeed, 'they' are just ordinary people, and none of them, repeat none of them, run this insane world. None of them want to destroy it or own it or kill it anymore than we want those things. They want to be left in peace to raise their families and live ordinary lives.

The fact is, the moment we nationally vilify others, we feel entitled to kill them, and let's face it, folks, this country is Murder Inc. USA. Our leaders control the killingest military force in the world. The American killing machine will go anywhere, anytime and kill anyone for any reason, for no reason at all, one at a time, in pairs, in mass numbers, in any variety and combination of ways, with or without torture, rape and disemboweling, with or without electrodes attached to genitals and breasts, and all at no cost to the supposed beneficiaries of all this killing. The American people, in semicomatose submission to the killer clown kings that lead this nation to endless war, will pay for every penny of it. They will pay for every bomb, every missile, every warhead, every bunker buster, every tank and plane and drone and concentration camp, every weapon and every drop of chemicals, every method of radiation and burning of flesh, and they will do so by and large while not having any idea about any of it. They will put themselves and their grandchildren seven generations forward into cast iron prisons of usurious debt that they will never, ever, ever be able to extricate themselves from, due to the illicit and unnecessary interest rates charged on all those hundreds of billions of dollars borrowed in order to keep on killing and killing and killing the whole damned world a hundred times over so that we can feel 'safe'. That's freedom, baby.

That's our biggest gift to humanity, folks, our bottomless hate-driven fear of brown people; go ahead and tell me I'm wrong. Americans love to hate. Not all of us by any means, but enough of us to do so much damage, it's hardly news. American bigots are ignorant, self-superior, hostile bullies that can be riled up and led as easily as exciting a kitten with a bit of string. All it takes is a concerted symphony of talking heads on TV spewing out hate and fear of people and love and respect for war, while pointing the finger somewhere 'over there' and saying, "We are in terrible danger, because those terrible people hate us and are going to come kill us in our beds!" That's all it takes, and boom! We're off to war. Again. And we're being seen naked and genitally groped in every airport in the country, because we are so afraid that maybe somehow somebody else might come along with another firecracker in his underpants and give us a good scare.

We can't handle it. We can't handle anything anymore, the whole damned world has become a direct threat to us. We're ready to kill everything anywhere anytime, just bring it on, because we're reduced to cowering whimpering fearful clinging followers of blatantly illegal, false, bloodthirsty authority that has made a total mockery of everything we are and everything we stand for and everything we believe in. We're fine with that, just don't let any of that evil socialism seep in here and don't let any of them towel-headed moozlums get us! Don't let them bring their America-hating God-hating women-hating Sharia law into our congress and force us to wear towel heads and beat our women and hate ourselves. Because that's just so likely to happen unless we wage war on the whole of the Muslim world and take all of their oil while we're at it and also pave the way for the infected carbuncle on the ass of the world known as Israel to move forward in their vision of Israel-World. More land for Israel. More and more and more land for Israel. Yes, they really need all that land. Would everyone in the Middle East please leave? Israel is moving in. And the US military contractors, agents and guns for hire are laying the sidewalk for them.

Is anybody really missing any of that? Really?

You know, me saying that, just calling it like I see it, if it came to the attention of the bigots and warmongers in control of our poor, castrated, confused country, would get me immediately branded as antisemitic and unpatriotic, and un-American, and maybe even as a terrorist supporter. Even though all I'm doing is reporting what is there to see, it is not hidden. I am telling the truth as I see it. How can that make me any of those things? Well, the short answer is, it can't. And it doesn't.

What is this about? All these attacks on people who won't tow the line of the illegal foreign corporate entity pretending to be our government? Why the brutality and bullying and forceful insistence that when we see what we see that it is not what we see, but something else entirely, that they will explain to us. These people are telling us what to think.

I don't need any help with how or what I think. I didn't ask for anyone's input on what I think. You don't get to dismiss me, I'm your equal bubba, deal with it. I see things different than the mindwashing sales pitch that's constantly being crammed down our throats. I think what they're selling is wrong. I think they lie about everything. And I think nothing they say deserves to override what the rest of us have to say. I know for sure that not one of those arrogant gas bags and phonies, dual citizenship senators, or pentagon denizens, or mass media propagandists is remotely qualified or entitled to tell me what to think. Every last one of them can kiss my big fat butt.

I will think what I think. I will say what I see. I will criticize the wrong-doing done in the name of this country. I will criticize the vile scum posing as our representation when we have so little real representation. Money talks and money walks, and money and guns are running our lives. Money and guns and a desire for domination so profound that it is the way it has always been on this poor little violence and greed ravaged world since forever. There's nothing new about this. This is the dark spot that goes round and round and round our world blocking out the sun and bringing on death and war and violence and rape and human sacrifice and pillage … all in the name of some authority or another. It's always the same people doing the same things.

The mighty, mighty mothersuckers are having their field day on earth, again. They want World War III so bad they can't stand it. They are working overtime like radioactive cockroaches scuttling about in the dark, in the walls, underground, with their tapped lines and intercepts, their media control, their plane loads of cash and prostitutes and hidden cameras, their illicit private contract killers, their bottomless funds, their legions of clueless youthful recruits to carry it all out for them, their well-honed needle sharp experts at manipulation, all working so hard, so relentlessly, every night and day, around the clock, to set Christians against Muslims, Jews against the world, to create armies of disgruntled head-shaving angry racists, masses of discontented, disillusioned, hopeless, grasping, hungry, homeless, jobless ordinary people, and stirring the pot, stirring the pot, turning up the heat. A steady stream of lighter fluid is added to the mix, and then one day, when the moon is in the right phase and the moment is right, they will simply toss in a single lit match, and it will explode into violent, earth-shattering hate and destruction. And mark my words, the self same creators of all of this hate and death and suffering will stand before us and look right into the television cameras to tell us that we have no choice but to nuke the shit out of whoever they'll say has done this to us. And we will say and do what we always say and do, "Hell, yeah! We're number one! We'll make them pay!"

Will anyone hear me telling them this is all contrived? It's all about money and power games and misguided sexual overdrive acting out a need to dominate everything that moves in order to feel secure that you'll get what you want and need and beyond. No, no one will hear me. In fact, I'll be branded unpatriotic, un-American, antisemitic, and a terrorist supporter, because I don't want to kill anyone. Because killing is not an answer, it is a depraved sport, and a lucrative sport at that, and I don't stand behind that or anyone who does. We have out of control murderers galloping the globe 'for God & country', for 'The Cause', which, as you know, means anything goes, anything at all in the name of 'The Cause'. And anything is going. Everything is going.

It all boils down to selfishness. And the delivery vehicle is so-called political correctness. I'm telling you that there are no such things as political correctness or preexisting conditions or the internet. There is only us. Just people. Plain, ordinary, human, mortal, imperfect people. People of all walks of life, all ages, all stages of health and sickness. Some are honest and honorable, some are wise, some are brave, and some are ignorant and small-minded. We're all just people. Our needs are the same no matter where we live: food and water, clothing and shelter, love and health and something meaningful to do with our lives. That's not hard to understand, is it? How can it be hard to understand that when people, any people, are systematically deprived of any of those things that there will be serious trouble?

All of the world's people have hearts and souls, we all love our children, and we all want to leave the world a better place. We all want to live in a just world, a fair world, a kinder world, a world without violence and armies and land grabs and power struggles. And if all of those mighty, mighty mothersuckers would just fuck off and leave the people of this world alone, we might just be okay. But they won't.

I say, don't hate your neighbor. Don't hate your neighbor if they have a problem with illegal immigration. Every country in the world is filled with people who react just like we do, when their borders are overrun with people from other places. It's not racist, it's a normal response. The feeling of being overwhelmed, overridden by strangers is scary and threatening. Massive immigration upsets the entire status quo. It uproots personal status and security, and if you don't think that's very serious indeed, then you just don't think. If you want to call that 'racist', then you need to get honest inside yourself.

People who are unhappy about illegal immigration, people of other faiths and cultures, people with other values and priorities than yours are not wrong, they are what they are, and who are you to judge them? Your position is not automatically right, why would it be? Would it kill you to take people as they are and love them anyway? No, but it will kill a lot of people if you don't.

Before you point at Muslims and exclaim they're crazed and violent extremists who hate us for no good reason, why don't you take a look at who is telling you those stories and who is benefiting from those stories being told? Because it isn't you, and it isn't me. It's the same old mighty, mighty mothersuckers who are raking in bottomless pits of benefits in dollars, the financial terrorists; plus their symbiotic enabling of the other mighty, mighty mothersuckers who forever lust to commit murder; mass murder for pleasure, mass murder as surrogate for sexual domination of the entire planet. Only the mighty, mighty mothersuckers benefit. Everybody else loses.

So please, spare me your judgment about my being and my person. I don't care if I'm not okay with you, I really don't. Your position is yours, and mine is mine, and if you will not shake my hand and be my neighbor anyway, then the real problem, my friend, is you.

Monday, January 24, 2011.

The Most Dangerous
Fundamentalist Extremists
in the World

If you want to find the real radical true believers, the real plotters of government takeovers, the real bomb-setting terrorists, the real haters of our freedom, the real killers of countless innocent people, then you'll need to look away from all of the usual places. It's not the Muslims. It's not the Christians. It's not the Jews. It's not any organized religion that you're aware of, yet it is the most powerful religion in the world. It is the religion of Doing Business.

Muslims, Christians and Jews have the same basic human values. They all believe in the sanctity of life. Life comes first. Protecting, nurturing and saving lives is held as the most important thing. Life is precious. Life is a miracle. Everything is done around and in support of life. But we ordinary people have very different values than the fundamental believers in Doing Business. Some who believe in the religion of Doing Business share these values too, but I'm not talking about them. The ones I'm talking about are the dangerous extremists who believe that you can kill your way to happiness, and they make it a regular part of Doing Business. When they Do Business, people get hurt.

Radical fundamentalist believers in Doing Business talk about all of the same values as we have and claim to hold them as their own, but there is one big difference that makes their value system a complete inversion of ours. That difference is the order of their values, what they hold in the highest esteem and will protect no matter what it takes. To these fundamentalist fanatics, the reason and purpose of life is Doing Business. Doing Business is the highest good. Doing Business is doing

God's work. Doing Business always comes first. Doing Business is the answer to all problems. Doing Business will set the world free.

This isn't economics, this is hardcore whacko fundamentalist religious belief. These are the most dangerous people in the world. They terrorize humanity and don't see a thing wrong with anything they do. They will always place Doing Business above protecting human life. Above protecting the environment. Above human rights. Above safety. Above human decency. Above justice. Above the law. Above common sense. Above freedom and democracy. None of those things will ever be allowed to stand in the way of Doing Business. Not anymore than you would be willing to let anything get between you and your religious beliefs.

For the radical true believers in Doing Business the fervor and excitement of Doing Business is all that matters. Doing business is everything. They love Doing Business. It is all they want to do. It is all they think about. It is all they care about. Everything else is unimportant. They're not necessarily pernicious, although they may be, but they are disconnected from anything that is not about Doing Business. They're not aware of anything beyond Doing Business. They believe that this world belongs to them and everything and everyone in it is either here to be exploited or it is in the way.

When you're doing business and something gets in the way, you find a way to get it out of the way. You have to get it out of the way or just plain get rid of it so that you can go on Doing Business. And if what you have to get rid of is some other country's leaders who believe that protecting, enriching and defending life comes first instead of Doing Business, then you do some business to have them taken out. You don't feel bad about doing this, it is how business is done. When you do business you bring prosperity wherever you go, and that means you are God's gift to this world. Any who stand in the way of God's work are evil, so removing evil-doers from the earth makes the world a safer and better place. You are absolutely entitled to destroy whoever and whatever is in your way, it is your God-given right. This is the same self-excusing logic that all fundamentalist extremist religious whack-jobs believe. It is exactly the same thing.

Now, not all the true believers in the religion of Doing Business are actually all that delighted about killing people. Many of them find it distasteful and ugly, and sad even. They would be truly hurt to be called heartless and uncaring. They would be outraged at being called terrorists or war criminals. They would say they feel sad when hundreds or thousands of indigenous farmers or peasants or modern city dwellers are killed or displaced and are suffering, starving or being tortured or blasted into bits by bombs and bullets, and so forth. They would say nobody enjoys seeing ravaged dead bodies, of course, it bothers them to see that. It gives them no pleasure, they are not beasts. But when they are trying to do business, to save the world through Doing Business, and people fight them, it must be dealt with. It's nothing personal. It's just Doing Business.

When they are trying to Do Business in Iraq or Afghanistan or anywhere in the world, and there are civilian casualties, this is a normal, reasonable and expected cost of Doing Business. The military, which Does Business as it's primary function, calls it 'collateral damage'. That makes it all right. It's not like they wanted innocent civilians to get killed, it is that it simply can't be helped sometimes. The military is there to Do Business, and the deaths of innocent people is one of the unfortunate costs of war. War is Doing Business. Since Doing Business is the most important thing, since it is the highest and noblest good, it is not wrong when innocent people die.

This is not an exception to the rules of Doing Business, it is a basic rule. This rule is in place all around us, it is common practice in every big corporate entity and plenty of small ones too.

Like when miners die in mine collapses because the mine owners refused to spend the money to make it safe for people to work in there, you and I would find that inexcusable and reprehensible.

Or when tons of contaminated 'No regulations' peanut butter horribly sickens or kills dozens of kids and adults and the peanut butter plant is not closed down or even fined after it gets inspected and is found to be teeming with scary health and safety hazards.

Or when airlines know about dangerous mechanical problems that need to be fixed, but they don't fix them, because they don't want to spend the money or lose revenues by taking airplanes out of service long enough to make the planes safe; then a plane crashes and hundreds of people die. You and I would see that as a preventable plane crash that should never have happened, and we would be furious. When you're doing business, you don't see things as you and I see things.

Here is how it goes in the corporate value system. Take the example of the preventable airplane crash. When executive officers are made aware of necessary safety enhancements, the first thing they do is call their accountants. The accountants crunch the figures on the costs of these safety enhancements. They take everything into consideration, not just parts, not just labor, but downtime too, because when a business has downtime, it is not Doing Business. When the final costs are determined, the accountants present the executives with the information. Regardless of the amount, the executives will also want to know how much it would cost them if they do not do the enhancements and there is a plane crash that destroys an airplane and kills everyone on board. The executives call their legal team to determine the amount of payments they'd have to make after the lawsuits that would be waged against the airline for the wrongful deaths of loved ones. Because the airplane is insured, losing a plane is not that big a deal, especially if it is nearing retirement. There would be some loss of revenue until the airplane could be replaced and put into service. There is also some cost associated with PR and damage control, and legal costs are considered, but since they have in-house lawyers, those costs are minimal too. Those costs are totaled and added to the total amount of the lawsuit payouts. Now, the projected cost of doing the repairs is compared to the projected cost of a plane crash. If it costs more to make the repairs to the fleet than it would cost to lose a plane and make survivor payouts, then the right thing to do is obvious. Don't make the repairs. Keep those planes flying. Letting a few planes crash is cheaper. It's just good business. It would be silly to do otherwise. Doing Business is the highest good. Lives lost are a secondary consideration.

That is the way it is. It is standard business procedure. It is not shocking. It is not bizarre. It is the norm. Companies will always tell you that everything they sell you is safe, that it is what they say it is, that it does what they say it does, and when what you get is not what they said it would be, you simply cannot be surprised. On the contrary, when you get what you pay for, then you can be surprised.

Tired of constantly paying for a new cell phone, because they break all the time? DVD and MP3 players that croak after a few months or are DOA in the box? Why is this so common and why don't they get their shit together? Well, here's why. After manufacturing a thousand electronic devices, if a company suddenly realizes the design has a defect and the devices are more than likely to fail, they are not going to trash them and start over. They are also not going to stop and go back and take the time to replace the known defective parts. Not all of the devices have those defective parts, maybe half or less. They are going to ship them to stores and deal with customer complaints later. That's why.

Three thousand people a year die in this country from food poisoning. Fifty million people a year in this country get food poisoning and survive. Removing the dang regulations to prevent all that food poisoning was just good business. When a production run of baby food tests with a too high level of some contaminant or another, they might not pull it. They'll find out how contaminated it is first, and unless it's ebola strength instant death, they'll just ship it out to stores. They know how unlikely it is that food poisoning, serious illness or death will be able to be tracked back to the source. If it happens, they'll deal with it then. Who cares? They have a business to run.

Despicable? Yes. Rare? Unfortunately, no. This is true with defective tires on cars, toxic dyes in clothing, lead in toys, poisonous fumes in carpets and paint, the list is literally endless.

The FDA routinely approves drugs that they know are killing people. A new tablet for indigestion causes a certain percentage of people to have a heart attack and die. They know this before the first box ships. It's been calculated three ways from sundown exactly how many people will die, how many people will suffer permanent heart damage, kidney damage, liver damage, etc., and out of those how many reports from physicians will be filled out and sent back to them. Those reports are how they do clinical drug trials now, by the way. They know only about ten percent of serious adverse reactions to drugs get reported back to them. Everything is on their side. It will take a very long time and tens of thousands of deaths before physicians themselves begin talking to each other and comparing notes and figuring out that the drug is killing people. Time is still on the drug makers side, because so few of the victims will be alive to sue them over it. When the drug company is finally accused of killing people again, they just deny it and walk away. The few really determined victims families and injured survivors who can somehow drag Big Pharma into court will still have to fight a long uphill battle against a company that has more money than God.

To the drug company, it really doesn't hurt a bit. They are making so much money selling people drugs they know do damage and cause death that it's not even funny. Who's going to stop them?

And folks, all drugs do some damage, that's just reality, not a news flash, a fact doctors knew back in the 1940s and people in general have always known. When you ingest anything that is not food, there will be a downside.

The bottom line is there is nothing whatsoever standing in the way of drug companies putting out anything they want. No matter what happens, they will get rich. And the FDA is there to support Doing Business, not to look out for you.

Dead mouse in a soda can? A rat in your KFC box? Duh. You have no idea what you may have eaten, and never knew. It's only when it's obvious enough to see it that you'd ever have a chance to know. They know. It happens. So what? What are you going to do about it? Nothing. They are home free. Every once in a blue moon somebody will take one of these huge corporations to court and win, but it ain't easy. And the media without exception portrays the injured American as a money-grubbing slime ball and the corporation as the victim.

The examples of these kinds of things are voluminous beyond number. But you get the idea. It's not the exception, it is the rule.

Now, back to the subject at hand. Here's the point. In case anyone out there hasn't noticed it yet, the most extreme, the most radical, the most insanely pious devotees of Doing Business have managed to take over our government. They go way beyond rat droppings in your cupcakes. These people are insane. Their religious zealotry and idealism has been bunker-bustered into the hallowed halls of the federal government through all three branches. Their doctrine is being taught in colleges and universities as economics, even though it flies in the face of long-held and proven standard economic theory and practice. Their economics are faith-based, not evidence-based. These guys are the penultimate believers in Doing Business.

In the year 2000, this faith-based economic system became our official state religion. Executive level government employees who refused to convert were dismissed from their careers and replaced by true believers. Jobs weren't given based on merit, but on true belief and willingness to serve. Dedicated, experienced government workers who had upheld the fair and honest business practices that kept things honest and reasonably accountable got laid off.

Lawyers and lobbyists worked hard to support Doing Business, and the congress turned into a whore house of business deals and business gifts like free trips to European golf vacations and corporate jets. Lobbyists handed out checks from people Doing Business to our elected representatives on the floor of congress, on live TV, as if it was perfectly normal and not criminal bribery. Our process of government was shamelessly bought and sold in acts of Doing Business as we watched in disbelief and horror.

Those first four years were the moment the church of Doing Business had prayed for all their lives. The believers were in ecstasy. Their arrogance and hubris beamed from their grinning faces. God was behind them all the way, and they knew it was true, because God was rewarding the followers of the scriptures of Doing Business with staggering profits and wealth. Their taxes were slashed and slashed again, all regulations were swept away, fraud was named a fair business practice and not a crime.

At last they were free to live the American Dream and prosper and Do Business with all the stops pulled out. Anything goes, and indeed, everything is gone. To the radical true believers the world was being saved right before their delirious eyes; they saw themselves as heroes and prophets, men amongst the most favored of God. "Our children will sing songs about us."

The holy doctrine of Doing Business was jack-hammered into every department of government and Doing Business, while those of us out here who do not believe in their strange religion felt sickened and horrified by the systematic destruction being wrought before our eyes, before the eyes of the whole world. These crusading zealots were and still are on a mission, one they worked hard to get started for many years. Now they have America in their hands and they are going to convert it, no matter what it takes, by force if necessary. They have Business To Do in the Middle East, and they wasted no time pushing America into war. They told us it would take six weeks and pay for itself, and the people there would shower our troops with flowers. But it was just the beginning of Total War, endless war, and with any luck, a world war of biblical proportion. That was the plan they wrote and published a year prior, and it was God's work.

Here on homeland soil, George W. Bush had his own to do list to accomplish. One of the earliest items he began to preach was globalization, public/private partnerships, privatization, which all mean the same thing. Doing Business by selling off public land, public resources and everything we think of as ours to rich people Doing Business all over the world. They've sold pretty much everything including our rights and our prosperity and our freedom and our health, the list is too long to mention here. Surrounded by ebullient, applauding true believers of his doctrine, the Patron Saint of Profit quickly blessed the torrential storm of contracting out to private business what the government is there to do. He privatized as much of what the government does as he could, including the most sensitive and top secret things, as well as the defense of our nation. Why do those things ourselves when we can Do Business and pay contractors exponentially more for doing work that we can't check or keep track of or verify? It was brilliant and perfect and great for America, he told us. The truest believers wanted to shrink the size of the government down where it would be small enough to drown it in a bathtub.

You wouldn't think it would be much of a surprise that with each passing year of his term in office more and more Americans hated what he was doing. They hated the corruption. They hated the lies, the manipulation, the insulting religiosity and attack dog mentality of Bush-supporting republicans. They were shameless and without conscience. They were out of control. They were doing incalculable damage, and somehow his followers couldn't see anything wrong. But objective and ordinary working class people were getting screwed and abused and ripped off and lied to and thrown under the bus, and they knew everything about it was wrong. The congress people who had rolled out the red carpet to these corrupt, insane zealots made America sick. The 2006 congressional elections made it perfectly clear. Congress people were thrown out of there in droves.

The zealots couldn't believe it. They were completely taken by surprise to find out that they weren't our dearest heroes who we adored and admired and agreed with. We saw them as criminals and scum, and they were sincerely shocked. But it didn't matter that we didn't want what they had to offer, and it didn't matter that we threw that batch out and put a new one in. Nothing changed. Nothing at all. It didn't even change when the whole republican party was thrown out the back door and spit on and told to go away and never come back. In fact, after Obama took office, things got worse and haven't stopped getting worse. The zealots never went away. They stayed out of sight just long enough to regroup and repackage the same message in a different way that people wouldn't recognize. Tea Party, people would support that. They want a Tea Party really bad. They want change they can believe in. These people were going to give us everything we wanted. They were not going to stop doing God's work no matter what the people want. The more angry the people get the more the zealots dig in.

The 'War on Terror' has morphed into more creative expressions of doing God's work, now including the terrible threat of terrorists that come from right here at home. Especially dangerous are those who are not in alignment with their radical religious beliefs, their political views, and even their personal opinions. Millions of Americans have been secretly investigated and their names added to lists of suspected terrorists, and those people can no longer get on an airplane. Last time I looked it was nearing one million names. Today they have to feel everyone's tits and crotch at the airport in order to keep us safe.

Fundamentalist extremist whack-jobs have driven America well into the belly of their beast. That belly is sacred too, by law. Anyone who doesn't agree with them is considered a likely terrorist. We live in a police state. Police no longer need warrants. We are no longer free. We are openly at war in at least four countries and secretly killing people in over 70 more countries. If these people don't like you, wherever you are, they're doing the business required to take you out. America is brain-dead and only a respirator is keeping the body warm. We need a miracle.

So when these people say that the human needs of Americans are superfluous and public money spent on health, education and human needs is wild and frivolous spending, they aren't kidding. Those who can't find jobs should not be rewarded with unemployment checks, they need to get up and Do Business. Those who cannot afford health care need to shut up and go Do Business. Old people are worthless and don't deserve anything. Doing anything to help those who do not Do Business is just plain evil. Social security is evil. Medicare is evil. Negotiating for lower prices for essentials is evil. Unions are evil. Taxpayers do not deserve to receive the benefit that comes of paying taxes. The most deserving recipients of tax benefits are those who are Doing Business. And the more successful and prosperous they are at Doing Business, the more they deserve the abundant rewards from our tax coffers.

Those who are unemployed, underemployed, elderly, disabled, sick, young or students are not doing anything to deserve benefits from the government. These are the people who deserve to bear the costs and tax burdens of the most prosperous, and so they are. When the big banks blew all of our hard-earned money gambling in con games for the rich, the government proclaimed they were too big to fail and gave them trillions of dollars, while Americans got kicked out of their homes. To them, this was noble and compassionate for these big banks had Done Business in a big way for a long time and now in a moment of need they deserved to be helped.

To put this in a slightly different perspective for the sake of contrasting the idiocy, imagine people coming to control of our government who had this same kind of over-the-top belief in and love of football, and their vision was a world of pro football stadiums holding pro football games in exclusion of everything else. Nothing else mattered. Everybody just needed to get up and get out there on that pro football field and play with everything they've got, and all of the world's problems will be solved. The fact that grandma can't even get out on the field and shouldn't have to doesn't matter to them. There is no room in their radical vision for any deviation. It is this or it is nothing. If you can't play pro football, you don't count. You're out. Nobody cares about you. That would cut out roughly half of America on the basis that we have babies, children, pregnant mothers, sick people, injured people, disabled people, students, people in hospitals, old people and people important to us who don't do mainstream things at all, like artists, writers, film makers, poets and spiritual leaders. But still, out of the remaining half of the people, how many would honestly have a chance of success out on their playing field with all of their insiders, important connections, huge dollars and humungous pro players who can easily play pro football and win? Are we really going to send pregnant women and people in wheelchairs out there? How about kindergartners?

The whole world cannot be about just one thing that some group of guys decide everybody else has to believe in as much as they do. That is the definition of insanity. It makes no sense. It is impossible. Plus it is just really-really creepy. But that's what selfish, arrogant radical extremists believe, and they don't care who doesn't like it. They decide they are right and you are wrong by decree. You don't get to have your own side. To them there is no other side. They are not sane or reasonable people. They have no respect for the vast majority of the people in this world, because very few people are able to get up on their private, exclusive playing field and join their game. And very few people are willing to give up what they love and believe in to redo the world in the vision of insane people who hate everybody who is not what they think everyone should be. That's simple reality. This is not hard. The fundamentalist radical response is that they will create their own reality. Don't they all try? And don't they all fail? But that's never stopped them from trying once again to kill their way to happiness. What they do is not about reason or reality or facts, it is about belief. They cannot be reasoned with. Reason and evidence will never touch them. These people do not believe in the sanctity of life. They are organized criminals and killers.

Are you getting the picture? It begins to make a lot more sense when you understand that what they seem to be saying is not really what they're saying. When they talk about national security and freedom and democracy, they are coming from a very specific and different place than we are. They are the exact opposite of everything we believe in. And they have robbed us blind, they have robbed the world blind, and they are galloping the globe spreading their religion with bombs and bullets, and they are sure they are heroes. They want to destroy this country and they want to destroy the European economy too. This horrendous destruction is serving them well. They have worked very hard to destroy everything we have all worked so hard and so long for, everything that has meaning and value to us. All of that has always been in their way. And in ten little years they've taken almost everything away. All that's left is grandma's monthly social security food money and what's left of a social safety net, and they're working on that right now.

If nothing else, know this. These people don't care about you. They don't care about us at all. They don't care if we die of hunger or if we are homeless or if we can't afford to see a doctor. They don't care. We are here for them to exploit and use and manipulate, and yes, even slowly poison to death with food and drugs and polluted water. It's all good. It's Doing Business, and we're all losers in their eyes. The question is, what are we going to do about it?

The first thing to do is to recognize the truth that they are very different than we are. This is something they have always known that we didn't know. This is something they have used to achieve their wildest successes without us understanding what was happening or why. They have always known how different their values are from ours. They know it very well. They know how we think. They know how we feel. They know what we want and what we believe in. They know what bothers us and what scares us. They also know that we didn't know the kind of people they are. We believed they were just like we are. We were not well-informed. That gave them one hell of a business advantage. Most of us could never believe that anyone could be so evil as these people, especially not our own government. Even today, with everything coming apart at the seams, many find it impossible to believe that they have been lied to and used and manipulated by people who know exactly what to say to appeal to our values and decency in order to screw us blind. It is time to climb up onto the back of that elephant in the living room to finally see the simple reality that the whole rest of the world can see. Our leaders are the most dangerous radical fundamentalist extremists on Earth.

It's not exactly that these 'leaders' are lying to us, they are often telling the absolute truth. It's just that it means the exact opposite of what we think it means. It is a cruel and sorry deception that is sadly our fault for not knowing about their kind. Their kind has been killing, enslaving and robbing humanity since before Christ was born. It is time for America to realize that we have nothing in common with these people. When America understands who and what these people are about, they will not be lied to anymore. It's really that simple.

There is nothing we can do to change these people. They cannot be changed. They are who and what they are. The only way that we can affect change is to educate others about this simple reality that is hidden in plain sight. Not knowing the difference between your friends and your enemies is extremely dangerous to your health.

Saturday, August 6, 2011.

I Wonder If....

I wonder if there would ever be another war if instead of mass slaughtering civilians, civilian homes, schools, and critical infrastructure, only heads of state would be bombed. If the innocent civilian populations of all countries were strictly off limits in times of war, not to be touched by violence or destruction, and instead only those directly responsible for war, those crying out and clamoring for war, would be the only ones targeted by the machines of war... I wonder, would we ever see another war? If only the presidential estates, the war think tanks, the political institutions, the highest seats of governments, parliaments and congresses were the sole targets of cluster bombs and land mines, if only the luxury homes and neighborhoods of the wealthiest and most powerful people were bombed to oblivion, if only the major corporations and major financial institutions and financial districts would be singled out for bunker busting, targeting by drones and D.U. munitions, which is only fair and right, because these are the people responsible for war; if this was the way that wars were fought, do you think we would ever see another war?

And what if the nation's capitol was in flames after being brutally bombed into ruins after white phosphorous bombs were liberally dropped from the sky and the guys in thousand dollars suits and ties were burning and screaming in agony (at least the ones who survived) along with the ladies in high heels wearing those huge Pebbles and Bam Bam pearl necklaces, if these utterly important worldly men and women were trapped and bleeding underneath smoking rubble, skin burning unstoppably, limbs torn off, brains on the walls, and if instead of sending in help we sent in heavily armed troops and police not to assist these people, but to point machine guns at them, at the politicians and heads of state, you know, to prevent looting. I wonder how well that would go?

I wonder if the bombed and injured politicians would applaud us and tell us we did the right thing in looking out for 'stuff' in the midst of incalculable human suffering and need instead of bending over backwards to save lives and help people. I'm sure they'd say it was the right thing to do. They've told us such behavior is the exact right thing to do, in Haiti, after Katrina, all over America, they've said so over and over again.

And what if we rounded up the filthy criminal bankers and corrupt liars and insiders and all of the cohort of official criminals and we hooded and shackled them, stripped off their clothes, gave them drug-filled enemas so they'd pass out and put them on airplanes, headed to points unknown, and twelve hours later we dropped them in a foreign country and left them there to be brutally tortured, anally raped with sticks and bottles and gun barrels, and hung from their wrists in some dark and filthy cell for days at a time without food, without medical attention, where they were beaten daily, and their bones were broken, and they were injected with drugs against their will and mentally tortured every minute of every day with no contact with the outside world and no hope, how do you suppose that would go over? Do you suppose the self same politicians who enabled the crimes and created these laws in the first place would still stand up for their laws and say, "It is good that you've done this to protect us all." Do you suppose that could ever happen?

And what if any of those banker criminals and their partners in crime in congress and the greater political cesspit began to protest, saying, "You can't do this to us! We have legal rights! We demand a trial! We demand a lawyer! We demand the right to defend ourselves! We demand to know what we are being charged with!" And we said, "Shut your face, you ain't getting any of that. You're guilty, because we say you're guilty. You're going to be in prison in a shithole getting tortured for the rest of your life, you ain't got no rights, you don't deserve the benefits of our precious American rights"... How do you suppose that would play out? Would the self-same politicians who created all of this in the first place say, "Righto! Well done! It's the best thing for our country! That's freedom and democracy, baby! That's genuine bona fide National Security!" Or, instead, might they mess their own pants in fear and panic that it was all turning around and coming back to them, to the people who created all of these despicable practices in the first place?

How can it be that we are supposed to see no hypocrisy in the way the rules apply to all of the equal beings in our free and democratic country? How can it be that some things are unthinkable wrongs when they are done to some people, but are heroic democratic patriotic goodness when they are done to others? Which is it? It can't be both. It is either good to do these things or it is bad to do them. Unless, of course, you believe that some people are better than others, so they don't deserve equal justice, they deserve to elude justice and be rewarded for their crimes while everyone else receives injustice and pays the highest price possible for crimes and misdemeanors, whether they are guilty or not. Is that free and democratic? Is that good and right and National Security and Law Enforcement O-Tastic goodness? Or is it total crap? I think it's grotesquely obvious total crap, but what I think is not the question. The question is: What do **you** think?

Wednesday, October 17, 2012.